Android TV
Apps Development

Building for Media and Games

Paul Trebilcox-Ruiz

Apress®

Android TV Apps Development: Building for Media and Games

ISBN-13 (pbk): 978-1-4842-1783-2

ISBN-13 (electronic): 978-1-4842-1784-9

Managing Director: Welmoed Spahr
Lead Editor: Steve Anglin
Development Editor: Chris Nelson
Technical Reviewer: Wallace Jackson
Editorial Board: Steve Anglin, Pramila Balan, Louise Corrigan, Jonathan Gennick,
    Robert Hutchinson, Celestin Suresh John, Michelle Lowman, James Markham,
    Susan McDermott, Matthew Moodie, Jeffrey Pepper, Douglas Pundick,
    Ben Renow-Clarke, Gwenan Spearing
Coordinating Editor: Mark Powers
Copy Editor: Kezia Endsley
Compositor: SPi Global
Indexer: SPi Global
Artist: SPi Global

Distributed to the book trade worldwide by Springer Science+Business Media New York, 233 Spring Street, 6th Floor, New York, NY 10013. Phone 1-800-SPRINGER, fax (201) 348-4505, e-mail orders-ny@springer-sbm.com, or visit www.springeronline.com. Apress Media, LLC is a California LLC and the sole member (owner) is Springer Science + Business Media Finance Inc (SSBM Finance Inc). SSBM Finance Inc is a Delaware corporation.

For information on translations, please e-mail rights@apress.com, or visit www.apress.com.

Apress and friends of ED books may be purchased in bulk for academic, corporate, or promotional use. eBook versions and licenses are also available for most titles. For more information, reference our Special Bulk Sales–eBook Licensing web page at www.apress.com/bulk-sales.

Any source code or other supplementary materials referenced by the author in this text is available to readers at www.apress.com/9781484217832. For detailed information about how to locate your book's source code, go to www.apress.com/source-code/. Readers can also access source code at SpringerLink in the Supplementary Material section for each chapter.

Contents at a Glance

About the Author ix

About the Technical Reviewer xi

■Chapter 1: Getting Started 1

■Chapter 2: Planning Your App... 9

■Chapter 3: Building a Media App 21

■Chapter 4: Enriching Your Media Apps 51

■Chapter 5: The Android TV Platform for Game Development 89

■Chapter 6: Android TV App Publishing 111

Index.. 117

Contents

About the Author ix

About the Technical Reviewer xi

■ Chapter 1: Getting Started 1

What Exactly Is Android TV? 1

What to Expect from this Book 2

Getting Set Up 2

Creating a New Android TV Project 3

Running Your Android TV App 5

Summary 8

■ Chapter 2: Planning Your App 9

Android TV Home Screen 9

Launcher Icon 11

The Recommendations Row 12

Global Search 14

User Experience Guidelines 15

Casual Consumption 15

Cinematic Experience 16

Keep It Simple 16

Designing Your Layout 16

Coloration 17

Using Text 17

Other Considerations 18

Summary 19

■Chapter 3: Building a Media App 21

Project Setup 21

Creating the Android Studio Project 21

Updating Dependencies 22

Building the Project Skeleton 23

Building the BrowseFragment Class 24

Creating the Data 25

Creating the Data Model 25

Loading the Data 27

Customizing the BrowseFragment UI 29

Creating a Presenter 32

Creating a Video Details Screen 34

Setting Up Video Details 34

Wiring Up Video Details 36

Displaying Content Details 37

Playing and Controlling Content 43

Creating the Media Player 43

Building the Playback Control Fragment 44

Creating Actions 47

Summary 50

■Chapter 4: Enriching Your Media Apps 51

In-App Searching 51

Adding a SearchOrbView 52

Creating the Local Search Activity and Fragment 54

Implementing Local Search from a Keyboard...56

Using Voice Input for Local Search 61

Implementing a Preference Screen...62

Displaying a Preference Item Entry Point 63

Creating the Preference Screen 66

Using Recommendations...71

Building Recommendation Cards 71

Starting the Recommendation Service...74

Android TV Global Search 77

Building the Search Database 77

Creating a Global Search Content Provider..82

Exposing the Content Provider 83

Reacting to the Search Action 84

More Media App Features 86

Now Playing Card 86

GuidedStepFragment...86

Live Channels 86

Summary...87

■Chapter 5: The Android TV Platform for Game Development........89

Android TV Games vs. Mobile..89

Manifest Setup 90

Gamepad Controller Input 90

Setting Up the Controller Demo Project...91

Storing Controller Inputs...93

Controller Best Practices 98

Using the Local Area Network 99

Setting Up a Second Screen Project..99

Advertising over the LAN 102

Discovering Over the LAN 105

Google Play Game Services 109

   Achievements 109

   Leaderboards... 109

   Saved Games... 109

   Multiplayer 110

   Quests and Events 110

Summary 110

■Chapter 6: Android TV App Publishing 111

Android TV App Checklist 111

   Support the Android TV OS 111

   UI Design 112

   Searching and Discovery.. 113

   Games.. 113

Distributing Your Application 113

   Google Play Store Distribution 113

   Amazon Fire TV Distribution 114

Summary 114

Index.. 117

About the Author

Paul Trebilcox-Ruiz is a software engineer on the emerging technologies team at Sphero, a Boulder, Colorado, based company best known for its work on a toy version of the Star Wars BB-8 Droid. Paul has a degree in computer science from California State University, Fresno. His main interests are in the Android platform, Android TV, and wearable computing. He also actively participates in hackathons in the Denver/Boulder area and writes Android technical tutorials.

About the Technical Reviewer

Wallace Jackson has been writing for leading multimedia publications about his work in new media content development since the advent of *Multimedia Producer Magazine* nearly two decades ago. He has authored a half-dozen Android book titles for Apress, including four titles in the popular Pro Android series. Wallace received his undergraduate degree in business economics from the University of California at Los Angeles and a graduate degree in MIS design and implementation from the University of Southern California. He is currently the CEO of Mind Taffy Design, a new media content production and digital campaign design and development agency.

Chapter 1

Getting Started

As we all know, technology is constantly progressing in every aspect of our lives. With the explosion of smart phones and tablets, it was only a matter of time before televisions joined the fray as one of the next connected "smart" devices. While interactive televisions have been around for a few years, major contenders have only recently entered the market, with Android TV having been introduced in June of 2014 (albeit after the failed attempt of Google TV and the huge success of Chromecast), and Apple TV finally opening their platform to app developers in September of 2015. Given this, now is the perfect time to prepare for the next trend in app development by expanding your skillset with Android TV.

What Exactly Is Android TV?

Android TV is an interactive television platform developed by Google and released at its I/O conference in 2014. Taking what Google had learned from one of their previous attempts at entering the living room, known as Google TV, they created this operating system to be easily embedded in television sets or to allow traditional "dumb" TVs to become interactive TVs through the use of standalone set-top boxes. The new platform is a version of Android that has been optimized for television, and has access to all of the features developers are already familiar with, as well as some additional components provided through the Leanback Support library.

In addition to being able to create native applications for Android TV, the operating system also provides support for Google Cast. Google Cast is familiar to most people as the technology behind the Chromecast. This means that if your existing application supports casting, then users will still be able to use it with the Android TV, though without the full immersive experience provided by having a native Android TV app. While understanding how to develop cast enabled apps is useful, this book will focus on developing native apps for Android TV.

What to Expect from this Book

This book is intended to get you started with the Android TV platform so that you can extend existing apps or create your own to improve the living room experience of your users. You should have a basic understanding of Android development, as you will be working with adapters, fragments, activities, views, and other standard Android components. Anything covered that has been specifically introduced for Android TV will be discussed in this book, so no previous knowledge of those components is required. As you work through this book, you will create a relatively simple Android TV media application by writing each of the components in order to fully understand how the application operates. You will also build a couple of small example programs that emphasize additional APIs, such as LAN communication and reading input from the game controller, so you can start to build other applications such as games and utility programs. Along the way you will learn design concepts related to what makes the user experience different on a television compared to smart phones and tablets.

By the time you finish reading this book, you should have a firm grasp on the vocabulary associated with Android TV. Not only will you be able to create apps for the platform, but you should also be able to confidently seek out answers to your more complicated questions by understanding what you are looking for when searching through forums and the extensive, well-written Android documentation from Google.

Getting Set Up

One of the nice things about developing for Android is that the development tools can be used on most modern computer platforms, and Android TV development is no different. For coding the examples in this book, you will need a computer running Windows, Mac OS X, or Linux. This book will focus on using Android Studio as the development environment, which itself currently requires the Java Runtime Environment (JRE) and Java Development Kit (JDK). If you do not already have Android Studio, you can get it and find the official system requirements, including minimum operating system versions, for Android development by visiting `https://developer.android.com/sdk/index.html`, downloading Android Studio, and following the installation instructions for your operating system. At the time of this writing, the latest version of Android Studio is 1.4. During the installation process you will need to install the platform tools and APIs for at least Android 5.0 (Lollipop).

Creating a New Android TV Project

Once you have installed and set up Android Studio, you can create a sample project using the base Android TV template provided by Google. Do this by opening Android Studio and clicking on Start a New Android Studio Project under the Quick Start header.

When you arrive on the Configure Your New Project screen, set the Application Name to Hello World, the Company Domain to apress.com, and your Project Location to wherever you want to save your source code (see Figure 1-1). Once you have filled in all of the required information, click Next and you will be taken to a screen to select which form factors your app will support.

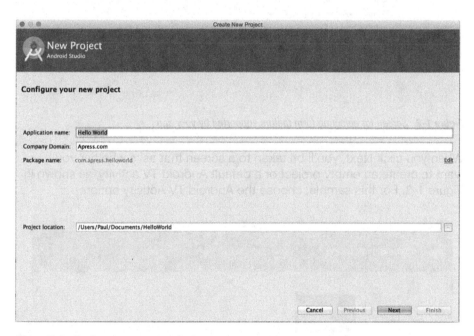

Figure 1-1. Configure your new project screen

For your Hello World application, unselect the check box next to Phone and Tablet and activate the check box next to TV. While you may have a module in your project for supporting phones and tablets, we will ignore that case for the sake of simplicity in this book. The minimum API version you will need for Android TV is at the oldest 21 (Lollipop), as Android TV was introduced with Lollipop. Figure 1-2 shows what your target Android devices screen should look like before continuing on.

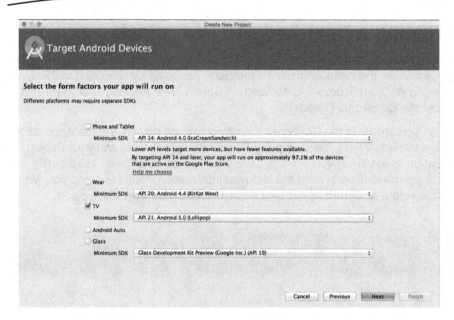

Figure 1-2. Screen for selecting form factors supported by your app

When you click Next, you'll be taken to a screen that asks whether you want to create an empty project or a default Android TV activity, as shown in Figure 1-3. For this sample, choose the Android TV Activity option.

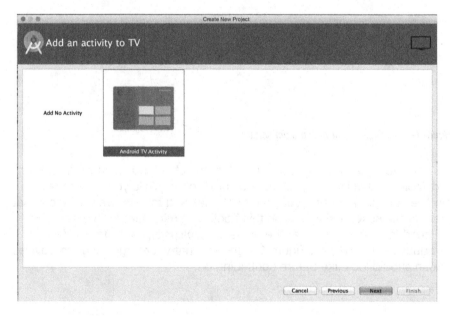

Figure 1-3. Selecting an Android TV template

The next screen you encounter will give you the option of renaming the activities, fragments, and layout files in the sample Android TV application (Figure 1-4). For this example, you can accept the default values and click Finish.

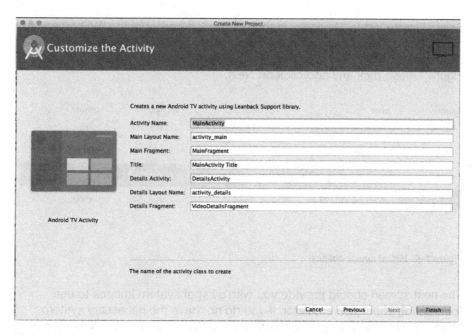

Figure 1-4. Naming your files

Android Studio will then take a moment to create the general template for your Hello World application. If you look through the source code for this application, you will notice over a dozen files just in Java. You may also notice that some of the files, such as VideoDetailsFragment.java, contain code that is deprecated, or no longer recommended for use by Google. For now, go ahead and ignore them as you will learn about the different recommended components for a media application later in this book.

Running Your Android TV App

The next step you will want to take is to run your Android TV app. As with mobile development, you can either use an emulator or install it on a physical device. In order to create an Android TV emulator, click on the AVD Manager button in the Android Studio toolbar (it will look like a phone screen with an Android head in the lower-right corner of the icon, and is the eighth button from the left in Figure 1-5).

Figure 1-5. Android Studio toolbar with AVD Manager button

Select Create Virtual Device… in the bottom-left corner of the AVD Manager
dialog that appears and select the TV category from the left column. There
should be multiple device profiles available to choose from, as shown in
Figure 1-6, so pick any and click on Next.

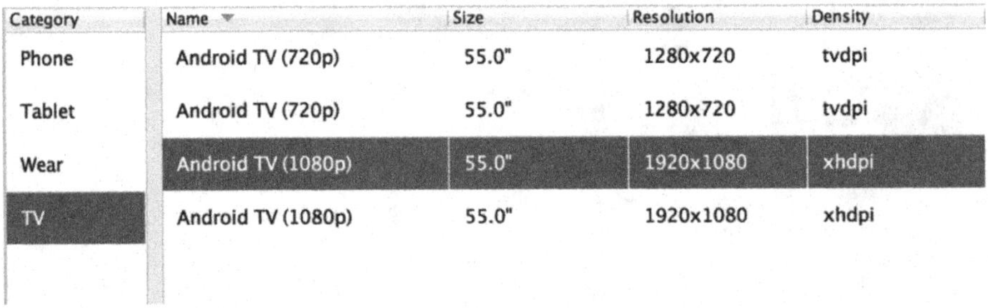

Category	Name ▼	Size	Resolution	Density
Phone	Android TV (720p)	55.0"	1280x720	tvdpi
Tablet	Android TV (720p)	55.0"	1280x720	tvdpi
Wear	Android TV (1080p)	55.0"	1920x1080	xhdpi
TV	Android TV (1080p)	55.0"	1920x1080	xhdpi

Figure 1-6. Virtual device options

The next screen should provide you with a list of system images to use
for creating your base emulator. If you do not have the necessary system
images on the next screen, check the Show Downloadable System Images
check box. You should see something similar to Figure 1-7. Download a
system image based on the Recommendation box on the right side of the
screen in order to build a virtual device that will perform well on your system.

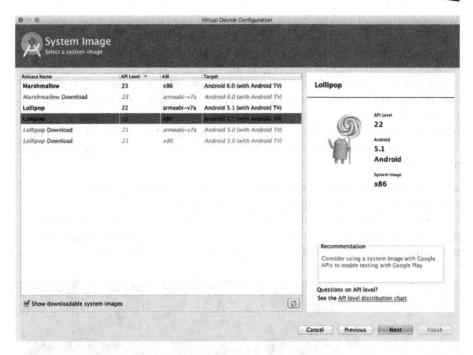

Figure 1-7. *Selection of system images for the Android TV emulator*

The last screen (shown in Figure 1-8) will give you the option to customize the virtual device settings. For these purposes, you can keep the defaults and click Finish to create your emulator.

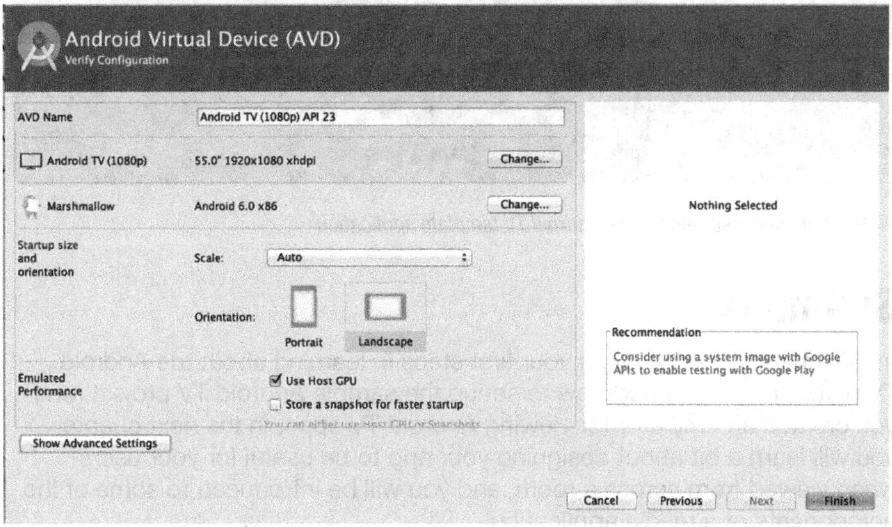

Figure 1-8. *Configuring your new Android virtual device*

While the emulator can be convenient, it is still best to test on a physical device. During I/O 2014, Google released a set of development devices that could be requested by developers, called the ADT-1. Once Lollipop was officially released, Google announced the Nexus Player, which is available for purchase. Other devices, such as the NVIDIA SHIELD, are also available from third-party manufacturers. As more OEMs integrate Android TV with their television sets or create set-top boxes, the selection of devices to test against will continue to grow. If you have a physical device to test with, you can simply plug the device into your computer while it is running to directly install your apps.

Now that you have a sample Hello World application created and an environment to run your application, click on the green Run arrow in the Android Studio toolbar to install your application to ensure that everything works. You should see a screen similar to Figure 1-9 when your application has launched in your emulator or on a physical Android TV device.

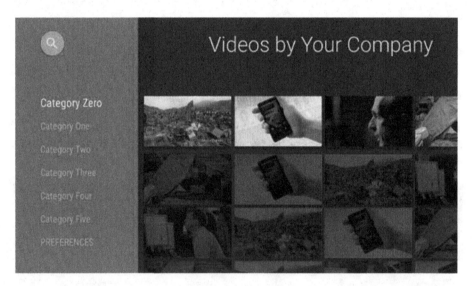

Figure 1-9. Initial screen for the Android TV template application

Summary

In this chapter you've taken your first steps in learning about the Android TV platform. You learned how to set up the sample Android TV project, and you created an emulator for viewing Android TV apps. In the next chapter you will learn a bit about designing your app to be useful for your users when viewed from across a room, and you will be introduced to some of the components of a media application.

Chapter 2

Planning Your App

Just like any movie or television show has to have a script, you should have a plan before you start programming an application. While you may be familiar with Android development for phones and tablets, there are many things you need to consider when creating content for the TV, depending on whether you are making a game, utility, or media application. In this chapter we will look at some of the design considerations that come into play when your users are experiencing your app from across a room rather than in their hands, and what you should think about when building your user interface to support the basic Android TV controller.

Android TV Home Screen

The first thing your users will see when they turn on their Android TVs is the home screen, which acts as the gateway to their televisions by providing various ways to discover content and interact with their apps. When applicable, you will want to take advantage of as many of these features as you can in order to make your app more visible to your users. At the very least, you will want to use an app icon specifically made for Android TV that easily identifies your app for your users.

The home screen is displayed to users in a row format that should look somewhat familiar from the Hello World application in the previous chapter (see Figure 2-1). The section above the top row contains the time and a Search button that can be selected or activated through the microphone button on a physical Android TV remote or in the official Android TV mobile remote control application from the Play Store (see Figure 2-2). The second row displays a list of recommended content generated from installed applications. Below the recommendations section are two rows—the top displays all installed applications that are not configured to be playable games and the bottom displays all games. Below the list of installed applications is the settings and system information row.

Figure 2-1. The Android TV home screen

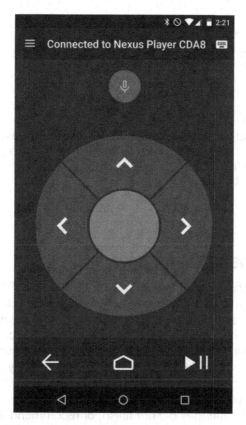

Figure 2-2. The Android TV remote control Android app

Launcher Icon

The most common way users will access your application is by selecting it from the list of installed apps on their TVs. This means that using a correctly sized and styled launcher icon is incredibly important for helping users find your application once it is installed on their devices. Since Android TV does not display the name of apps below their icons, you must include the name of your app in the launcher icon. Your launcher icon should be sized at 320px x 180px in order to be displayed correctly by the home screen. Once you have an asset created for your launcher icon, you will need to apply it to your launch activity in your `AndroidManifest.xml` file similarly to a standard Android application. It should be noted that the category option will use a `LEANBACK_LAUNCHER` instead of a standard `LAUNCHER` in order to display the TV launcher icon. If you are building a game, you will also need to add the `isGame="true"` property to the application node so that the home screen places your launcher icon in the games row.

```
<application
        android:label="@string/app_name"
        android:icon="@mipmap/ic_launcher"
        android:theme="@style/AppTheme">
        <activity
            android:name="MainActivity"
            android:label="@string/app_name">
            <intent-filter>
                <action android:name="android.intent.action.MAIN" />
                <category android:name="android.intent.category.LEANBACK_
                LAUNCHER" />
            </intent-filter>
        </activity>
</application>
```

The Recommendations Row

The recommendations row is the first row on the Android TV home screen, as seen back in Figure 2-1, and is the easiest way to gain user interest for your app. There are three categories of content that a developer can recommend: continuation, related, and new. When you create the list of recommendations from your app to be displayed on the home screen recommendations row, you should determine what to display based on relevancy to past consumption behavior. If your users previously watched a show in your app, you can present a continuation recommendation that displays an episode that they did not finish, or recommend the next episode in that show. You can also display a related recommendation that introduces new content that your user may enjoy based on previously viewed media. The last type of content that can be recommended falls under the new category. This is an excellent spot to highlight featured media and introduce content that your users may enjoy. When displaying new content recommendations, you should be careful not to accidentally give away any spoilers that may ruin interest. You should also be mindful with related and continuation recommendations, as the related row is visible to all users on the Android TV, and therefore should be appropriate for all ages.

Android TV uses a simple and easy-to-digest card format across the platform for displaying information to users, as seen in Figure 2-3.

Figure 2-3. *Recommendation card. The number 1 designates the large icon, 2 is the title, 3 is the content text, and 4 is the small icon*

While this format is already set for you, you still have the ability to customize the cards to fit the feel of your own application. Each card contains of a single display image that should describe the recommendation at a glance. This display image should be 176dp or higher height, and the width should be in a ratio of 2/3 to 4/3 the height. When the users scroll over the recommended content, the highlighted item will expand to display the rest of the card. You can change the card background color, though it should complement white text well. You will also want to add a small icon to the card that represents your application. This small icon should be a 16dp x 16dp PNG with a transparent background and foreground in #EEEEEE.

There are two pieces of textual information that you can display with a recommendation card: a title and a content text. The title should be the primary descriptor for the content, such as a song or movie title. The optional content text is where you can tell your users some information about the content, such as why it is being displayed to them. One example where the content text may be useful is when displaying a video feed from a sporting event. If the event is currently in progress, or if the event has already finished and you can play back a recording, are excellent pieces of information that users may want to know about and interest them enough to open your app.

In addition to the display card, you can also change the background on the home screen based on the highlighted recommendation. This not only allows you to give your app recommendation a stylish piece of flair, but also provides another way to intrigue your users by giving them more information about the content. Using large background images to paint a picture for your users can go much further in gaining their interest than a paragraph describing the content. This image should be 2016px x 1134px (1920 x 1080 with a 5% margin), and different than your standard display image. It should be noted that if the image is not sized correctly, the system will attempt to scale it to fit, which may have undesirable consequences, such as lower image quality.

Once your users have started viewing media from your app, you can provide a Now Playing card that looks identical to a standard recommendation card, but also includes a progress bar. Not only does this card provide useful information to your users, but it also appears as the first card in the recommendation row, helping maintain user engagement. When used well, the recommendations row provides a powerful way to get users to open your app as they see what content is available to enjoy. Later in this book you will learn how to implement a simple recommendation service in a working media application.

Global Search

When the users have some idea of what they're looking for, such as a specific movie, it can be cumbersome to find an app that has that content available. Luckily, Android TV provides a search option that can search across multiple apps at the same time so users can quickly find what they are looking for. By pressing the microphone button on the remote control app, or by navigating to the search globe at the top of the home screen, users can enter into a search UI where they can say or type in what they're looking for (see Figure 2-4). When the user performs the search, all apps that are searchable on the Android TV will run the query and return related content, if any. Once the results are shown to the users, they may be selected to link directly to the desired media. By making your application searchable, you can add visibility to your app in order to drive user engagement.

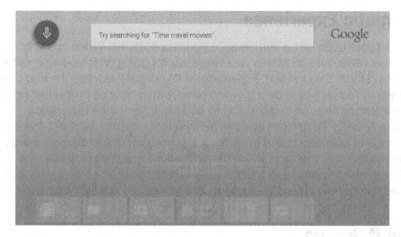

Figure 2-4. Android TV home screen search box

User Experience Guidelines

Now that you are aware of how you can use the home screen to draw users to your app, you will need to have a well-designed app that is easy to use and visually appealing in order to keep them engaged. It is important to realize that televisions have been around for a lot longer than smart phones and tablets, so users come with a predefined expectation on how their experience with the television should go. Google recommends that your apps follow three main ideas: allow for casual consumption, provide a cinematic experience, and keep things simple.

Casual Consumption

The key difference between a smart phone or tablet and the television is that the television is designed to be used specifically as an entertainment device. In order to fit into the ideal use-case for the TV, you should understand the overall goal of your application and help your users reach that goal as quickly as possible. If your application is meant to display media, then you should design your app to only take a few clicks to get to content that your users would want to see and start playing it. If you are building a game, then you should give your users an immersive experience that lets them play your game without distracting them with a lot of content not directly related to gameplay. Applications that are geared toward interacting with multiple people in a single room, such as a party game or karaoke app, should provide the users with information they need while letting them focus on the more important thing, the other people in the room.

Cinematic Experience

You want your users to be immersed in your applications. When possible, use audio and visual cues to inform your users what's going on in your app rather than telling them through text. For example, if your user reaches the end of a list, Android tends to provide a glowing effect with a bounce on the last item. You can also provide an audible *ding* to add more flair to the experience. Because Android TV devices all run a minimum of Lollipop (SDK 21), there's a wide range of animations and transitions that you can use to delight your users as they go through your app. While the animations may be enjoyable, you should attempt to provide as much content as possible on each screen and limit the number of screens your users have to view in order to reach their goal.

Keep It Simple

This is the most important of the design guidelines, and the overarching theme when it comes to designing for Android TV. When your users sit down in front of their televisions, they want to be able to quickly find something to watch or start playing a game. In order to help out your users, keep the number of screens between entering your app and enjoying content to a minimum. Try to avoid requiring any kind of text entry, and always provide a voice input option in those situations where you must enter data. Remember that most users will interact with their TVs using a simple D-pad controller with a selection button from either a remote included with their Android TV or from the remote control app. UI patterns should be easy to navigate with only a few available buttons. Make sure you do not just copy the UI from a touch screen device, but instead try to use the list of rows pattern as seen on the home screen. What works on phones and tablets may not translate well to the television. The simpler your application, the happier your users.

Designing Your Layout

One of the most defining factors between what feels like a well or poorly designed app for the television is how cluttered the screen looks. How you space out your content, how many items are on the screen, and the size of those items all contribute to the cleanliness of your UI. While televisions continue to get larger and support higher resolutions, it is always better to stick to fewer visible items that are of higher quality than many items that are not as appealing. All of your layouts should always be designed to work in landscape mode, as most home televisions do not support portrait viewing. Along these same lines, any navigation UI components should occupy the left or right of the screen so that vertical spacing can be saved for displaying content. Finally, you should always ensure that you have enough margin space so that items are not against or outside the edges of the screen.

The general rule is to add 10% margins to the edge of your layout to account for overscan, which is an area of the television that may be outside of the visual borders of the screen. While this may seem like a lot to account for, if you're building a media playback app the Android Leanback Support library already takes the layout design guidelines into consideration and handles them for you.

Coloration

While computer monitors and mobile devices tend to be fairly consistent when displaying colors across different devices, televisions do not offer that luxury and special precautions should be taken when choosing colors for your apps. Different types of TVs, such as plasma or LCD, may vary in how they display colors due to inherent properties of the technology or applied sharpening and smoothing filters. On top of that, subtle differences in brightness or hue can be either indistinguishable or over-emphasized on some devices. Avoid using the color white (#FFFFFF) on large areas of the screen, as it can be harsh on eyes when displayed on a bright screen. You should also check very dark or highly saturated colors against various televisions and settings to ensure they meet your expectations. Google recommends using a color that is two to three levels darker than those used on a mobile device. It also suggests choosing colors from the 700-900 range from the Google color palette found at `www.google.com/design/spec/style/color.html#color-color-palette`.

Using Text

While text should generally be avoided to maintain an immersive experience, there will be a few places where it is a necessity. Given that users on average sit roughly ten feet (three meters) away from their television sets, styling text so that it is readable is important. You will want to break text into small chunks so that it is easy to read. Text should be preferably a light color on a darker background and you should avoid thinner fonts like Roboto Light, for example, since television settings may make them unreadable. While the smallest size you should use is 12sp, the recommended default size for Android TV is 18sp. Google has also put together a set of recommended sizes for different sections of a media app:

- Titles on cards should use Roboto Condensed at 16sp

- Subtitles on cards should use Roboto Condensed at 12sp

- Titles on a browse screen should use Roboto Regular at 44sp

- Category titles on a browse screen should use Roboto Condensed at 20sp

- Content titles on a media detail screen should use Roboto Regular at 34sp

- Description text on a detail screen should use 14sp

You should notice that all font sizes are listed in *sp,* which is a density-independent sizing quantifier specifically for text. This allows the operating system to determine what size is appropriate on a given device. While this may seem like a lot to remember, the Leanback Support library classes contain their own styles that will handle that logic for you.

Other Considerations

While understanding design guidelines is important, there are other things that you need to consider before building your application.

- If you are building a game for Android TV, you may want to investigate Google Play Game Services, as Google has put together an impressive set of utilities to make game development faster and easier: developers. google.com/games/services/.

- If you are building a media application, you should think about where your media is coming from. Are you hosting all content on your own server, or are you aggregating multiple services? How do you handle contingencies like no Internet connection, or a server not returning content? You will also need to think about how your content is formatted to ensure that it can be played back on an Android TV device. You can find a list of supported media formats for Android on Google's official documentation page: developer.android.com/ guide/appendix/media-formats.html.

- If your content is through a proprietary third party that requires the use of its own media player software, you will need to ensure that it supports the use of the Android TV D-pad controller.

- If you need to support Digital Rights Management (DRM), then you may find the Android DRM documentation useful: source.android.com/devices/ drm.html.

Once you are aware of all of your requirements, you can choose how you will display your content. While your requirements may exclude the possibility, Google does offer an excellent open source media player called ExoPlayer that supports features not currently available in the `MediaPlayer` class: `developer.android.com/guide/topics/media/exoplayer.html`.

While these topics are beyond the scope of this book, they are important to review to make sure your time is well spent when developing your final product.

Summary

In this chapter you learned about the various sections of the Android TV home screen and how to catch the interest of users for your app. You also learned about design principles in relation to Android TV and the recommendations from Google for making your apps visually appealing. In the next chapter you will begin building a very basic media playback application to learn about some of the key parts of the Leanback Support library, and how you can use them to build an Android TV app.

Chapter 3

Building a Media App

Without a doubt, the most common type of application that developers create for televisions simply display and play media. Knowing this, Google has created the Leanback Support library, which provides common components for creating apps that fit perfectly within the design guidelines for Android TV. In this chapter you will start creating a basic media app from the ground up in order to learn about a few of the components available for creating a simple and enjoyable experience for your users.

Project Setup

When you created the Hello World application in Chapter 1, you probably noticed that the sample application is fairly large, and you more than likely saw some warnings about the use of deprecated classes in areas like the content details fragment. In order to have a better understanding of what goes into creating a media app without sifting through the clutter, you will create one piece by piece from a blank slate. While there is a lot more that can be done to really make the app shine, this book focuses on the essentials in order to teach the topic without getting bogged down in details that are best left as a fun exercise.

Creating the Android Studio Project

Start by opening Android Studio and getting to the Welcome to Android Studio screen. Generally this will be the first screen you see when you open the program, but if you previously had a project open (such as Hello World), then you will need to close it to return to the Welcome screen. Click on Start a New Android Studio Project in the right panel to be taken to the Configure

Your New Project screen. In the Application Name field, enter Media Player and enter apress.com for the Company Domain. Pick a path for Project Location and then click on Next.

On the next screen, you will need to pick the form factors that your app will support. For Media Player, select TV and set the Minimum SDK to API 21: Android 5.0 (Lollipop). On the same screen, deselect the Phone and Tablet item and then click Next.

In Chapter 1, you had Android Studio create an Android TV activity, which in turn created an entire Android TV demo application. For the Media Player application, click on Add No Activity and then click Finish. When Android Studio creates the project, you will have the base structure for your app, but it will be mostly devoid of source files.

Updating Dependencies

The first thing you will want to do is open the build.gradle file. While a detailed look at the Gradle build system is out of scope for this book, you will only need to use it for adding dependencies in this project. In the Dependencies node, you should already see lines that import the Leanback Support library and the RecyclerView library. You will also need to import the GSON library, which you will use for creating objects from JSON data, and the Picasso library from Square, which is used to easily display images in the app from the Internet. Each item shown in the following code listing is the latest version of the libraries at the time of this writing.

```
dependencies {
    compile fileTree(dir: 'libs', include: ['*.jar'])
    compile 'com.google.code.gson:gson:2.3'
    compile 'com.squareup.picasso:picasso:2.5.2'

    compile 'com.android.support:leanback-v17:23.0.1'
    compile 'com.android.support:recyclerview-v7:23.0.1'
}
```

> **Tip**   Square offers a wide variety of open sourced libraries that can be useful when creating apps. You can find a list of their released libraries at http://square.github.io/.

Building the Project Skeleton

Once you're done updating build.gradle, navigate to app/src/main/java in the left navigation panel if you are in the Project navigation layout (app/java if you're in the Android navigation layout). In Android Studio, right-click on the package name, go to New and Java Class. Name your new Java class MainActivity and click OK. You will want MainActivity to extend Activity and then you will override onCreate to associate the activity with a layout file.

```java
public class MainActivity extends Activity {
    @Override
    protected void onCreate(Bundle savedInstanceState) {
        super.onCreate(savedInstanceState);
        setContentView( R.layout.activity_main );
    }
}
```

MainActivity will be the first activity that your users will see when they enter your app. As such, you will need to declare it in AndroidManifest.xml and denote it as the main and launching activity.

Finally, you will need to add three lines to the top of AndroidManifest.xml within the manifest tag. The first declares that the application needs to have the INTERNET permission. The next two state which features are required by the device for using the app. In this example, you will set the app so that a touchscreen is not required, but the Leanback feature is. This will make it so your app will be installable on Android TV systems.

```xml
<manifest xmlns:android="http://schemas.android.com/apk/res/android"
    package="com.apress.mediaplayer">
    <uses-permission android:name="android.permission.INTERNET" />
    <uses-feature
        android:name="android.hardware.touchscreen"
        android:required="false" />
    <uses-feature
        android:name="android.software.leanback"
        android:required="true" />
    <application android:allowBackup="true" android:label="@string/app_name"
        android:icon="@mipmap/ic_launcher" android:theme="@style/AppTheme">
        <activity
            android:name="MainActivity"
            android:label="@string/app_name"
            android:logo="@mipmap/ic_launcher">
            <intent-filter>
```

```
                    <action android:name="android.intent.action.MAIN" />
                    <category android:name="android.intent.category.LEANBACK_
                    LAUNCHER" />
               </intent-filter>
          </activity>
     </application>
</manifest>
```

Now that your manifest is set up, you will need to create a layout file for MainActivity. Right-click on app/src/main/res in the left navigation pane of Android Studio (again, assuming you are in the Project navigation layout) and create a new Android Resource Directory called layout. Next, you will need to right-click on layout and create a new Layout resource file called activity_main. This layout file will consist of a single item.

```
<?xml version="1.0" encoding="utf-8"?>
<fragment xmlns:android="http://schemas.android.com/apk/res/android"
     android:id="@+id/main_browse_fragment"
     android:name="com.apress.mediaplayer.MainFragment"
     android:layout_width="match_parent"
     android:layout_height="match_parent" />
```

You will notice that this fragment uses the name property to point to com.apress.mediaplayer.MainFragment. MainFragment will be an extension of the BrowseFragment class, which is provided by the Leanback Support library. BrowseFragment will allow you to display rows of items representing the content of your app, preferences, and a search option. Create MainFragment now by right-clicking on your app package name under app/src/main/java and creating a new Java class called MainFragment. Once the file is created, make it extend BrowseFragment.

```
public class MainFragment extends BrowseFragment { }
```

At this point you should be able to run your application without any problems, though it will only display a black screen with a teal panel (called the fast lane) on the left side. Next you will begin building out the BrowseFragment class, which will use a local data file and model to display cards using a presenter.

Building the BrowseFragment Class

Provided by the Leanback Support library, the BrowseFragment class makes up one of the core parts of an Android TV media app. While it acts as a single fragment in use, it is actually composed of two fragments: a RowsFragment and a HeadersFragment. The RowsFragment displays rows of customized cards representing your content, and each row has a header above it that is typically used for displaying a category name. Those headers are also used to populate the HeadersFragment, which makes up the teal fast lane panel that you see when you run the application up to this point.

Creating the Data

Before you start working in your BrowseFragment, you will need to plan out the data for the content that you want to display to your users. In a production app, you would more than likely want to store this data somewhere online or have an API that delivers the data to your app so that you can easily deliver new content or adjust what your users see based on their use habits. In order to reduce complexity and focus on the Android TV platform, the Media Player app that you are building will simply store the content data in a JSON file within the app and read that into the BrowseFragment. A sample data file can be found with the code samples of this book in the Data folder. Each item in the JSON array represents a different movie in the public domain. The fields used for this tutorial are "title," "description," "videoUrl," "category," and "poster". If you would like to use your own content or add your own to the data, you just need to follow this item format:

```
{

    "title": "Content title",
    "description": "Some long text description",
    "videoUrl": "Video URL",
    "category": "Category",
    "poster": "Image file URL"
}
```

> **Note**   The movies used in the sample data are all in the public domain, and the video files used for playback are hosted by archive.org, a non-profit Internet archive of public domain content.

Once you have your data file, name it videos.json and place it in a new directory named raw under /app/src/main/res.

Creating the Data Model

Next you need to create a model object class that represents the data for use in the app. This model will need to implement Serializable in order to turn the data into a string representation that can be passed between components in the app. You will also use the GSON library from Google in order to take the JSON file and easily parse it into a list of objects, so you will need setters and getters for each of the properties in the model.

Create a new Java file under your app package folders in the app/src/main/java directory and name it Video. Once Video.java is created, add the strings for each of the data properties, the toString method, and the getters and setters, as shown here.

```java
public class Video implements Serializable {

    private String title;
    private String description;
    private String videoUrl;
    private String category;
    private String poster;

    @Override
    public String toString() {
        return "Video {" +
                "title=\'" + title + "\'" +
                ", description=\'" + description + "\'" +
                ", videoUrl=\'" + videoUrl + "\'" +
                ", category=\'" + category + "\'" +
                ", poster=\'" + poster + "\'" +
                "}";
    }

    public String getTitle() {
        return title;
    }

    public void setTitle(String title) {
        this.title = title;
    }

    public String getDescription() {
        return description;
    }

    public void setDescription(String description) {
        this.description = description;
    }

    public String getVideoUrl() {
        return videoUrl;
    }
```

```
    public void setVideoUrl(String videoUrl) {
        this.videoUrl = videoUrl;
    }

    public String getCategory() {
        return category;
    }
    public void setCategory(String category) {
        this.category = category;
    }

    public String getPoster() {
        return poster;
    }

    public void setPoster(String poster) {
        this.poster = poster;
    }
}
```

Loading the Data

Now that you have a model representing the data, you can use it in your BrowseFragment. The first thing you need to do is create a list of Video objects at the top of the MainFragment class in order to store your data.

```
private List<Video> mVideos = new ArrayList<Video>();
```

Next you should override the onActivityCreated method, as this will drive most of the logic in the fragment. Within onActivityCreated you should call loadData, which is a helper method that you will create in order to load data into mVideos.

```
@Override
public void onActivityCreated(Bundle savedInstanceState) {
    super.onActivityCreated(savedInstanceState);
    loadData();
}
```

Before you can define loadData, you should create a new Java class in your application package folder called Utils. Utils will contain a static method named loadJSONFromResource that accepts a context and a resource ID for a local JSON file, in this case videos.json, so that it can be converted into a string and returned. Enter the following code into the Utils package and then return to MainFragment.

```
public class Utils {

    private Utils() {}

    public static String loadJSONFromResource( Context context, int resource ) {
        if( resource <= 0 || context == null )
            return null;
        String json = null;
        InputStream is = context.getResources().openRawResource( resource );
        try {
            if( is != null ) {
                int size = is.available();
                byte[] buffer = new byte[size];
                is.read(buffer);
                json = new String(buffer, "UTF-8");
            }
        } catch( IOException e ) {
            return null;
        } finally {
            try {
                if( is != null )
                    is.close();
            } catch( IOException e ) {}
        }
        return json;
    }
}
```

Now that you have a method for reading in the JSON file that you created earlier, it's time to use it. Create a new method called loadData in MainFragment and have it generate a string from Utils.loadJSONFromResou rce. Next you will need to use reflection and the GSON library to populate your list of video objects so that they can be used for populating your BrowseFragment UI.

```
private void loadData() {
    String json = Utils.loadJSONFromResource( getActivity(), R.raw.videos );
    Type collection = new TypeToken<ArrayList<Video>>(){}.getType();

    Gson gson = new Gson();
    mVideos = gson.fromJson( json, collection );
}
```

When you have finished loading the data into your fragment, you can start diving into creating the UI for your Android TV media app. In the next section you will set some UI properties for the BrowseFragment and then use the list of videos that you just generated to create rows of customized cards that you can click on to get to the video detail activity.

Customizing the BrowseFragment UI

If you read over the BrowseFragment documentation page from Google (developer.android.com/reference/android/support/v17/leanback/app/ BrowseFragment.html), you'll notice that there are several methods available for customizing some of the UI aspects of the fragment. For the sake of simplicity, we'll only cover a few of them here. In onActivityCreated, below your call to loadData, add the following three lines

```
setTitle( "Apress Media Player" );
setHeadersState( HEADERS_ENABLED );
setHeadersTransitionOnBackEnabled( true );
```

Each of these methods controls a different customizable part of the BrowseFragment UI:

> The setTitle method will take the string passed to it and display it in the upper-right corner of the BrowseFragment.

> Using setHeadersState accepts one of three predefined values in BrowseFragment that will allow you to control how the HeaderFragment fastlane works. HEADERS_ENABLED leaves the fastlane usable and expanded, HEADERS_DISABLED will hide and disable it (see Figure 3-1), and HEADERS_HIDDEN will enable the HeaderFragment while mostly hiding it except for a sliver on the side of the screen.

> Finally, while the headers transition on back operation is enabled by default, I have included it here because it is important to point out. When the user opens the HeadersFragment, an entry will be added to the back stack. This means that when the user presses the back button on their controller, the headers section will transition. If you want to override the back button operation, you will need to call setHeadersTransitionOnBackEnabled with a value of false, and then override BrowseTransitionListener for implementing your own back stack handling.

Apress Media Player

Figure 3-1. BrowseFragment with hidden fast lane

Now that you have set some of the BrowseFragment UI properties, it's time to add rows of cards for your data. The way BrowseFragment displays rows of content is by taking an ObjectAdapter and displaying lists of content (rows) in a vertical list. Each item in a row is associated with a Presenter object that defines how each item will look in the UI, which in this case will be a card with an image and film title. Above each row will be a title representing the categories for the videos in your data set.

In the onActivityCreated method of MainFragment, add a method call to a new helper method named loadRows with no parameters. Next you will define loadRows. The first line in the new method will initialize an ArrayObjectAdapter with a ListRowPresenter that will contain each of the rows. ListRowPresenter is used to define how a row of items will work in the BrowseFragment. After initializing ArrayObjectAdapter, you will want to create a new object called CardPresenter. CardPresenter is a class that you will create later in this section, so for now you can ignore the error that Android Studio gives you.

```
private void loadRows() {
    ArrayObjectAdapter adapter =
        new ArrayObjectAdapter( new ListRowPresenter() );
    CardPresenter presenter = new CardPresenter();
```

Next you will need to create a list of string objects representing the categories of your videos. Each of these categories will be used above a row to help organize your content for your users. Here you will use another helper method named getCategories that will loop through each video item in the data and add its category to a list. While this may not be the most efficient way to create the categories list, it's suitable for the purposes here.

```
List<String> categories = getCategories();
if( categories == null || categories.isEmpty() )
    return;
```

where getCategories is defined as

```
private List<String> getCategories() {
    if( mVideos == null )
        return null;
    List<String> categories = new ArrayList<String>();
    for( Video movie : mVideos ) {
        if( !categories.contains( movie.getCategory() ) ) {
            categories.add( movie.getCategory() );
        }
    }
    return categories;
}
```

Now that you have a list of categories, you can create cards using the CardPresenter class and add them to rows in the BrowseFragment based on the category of each data item. For simplicity, you will loop through the list of categories and check each data item to see if the category matches. If it does, you will add it to a new ArrayObjectAdapter. Once all of the movies for a category are added to the new adapter, you will create a new HeaderItem and use that with the ArrayObjectAdapter to create a new row of items. Finally you will call setAdapter, a method built into BrowseFragment, to add the parent ArrayObjectAdapter that you created first in loadRows as the main adapter for the fragment.

```
for( String category : categories ) {
    ArrayObjectAdapter listRowAdapter = new ArrayObjectAdapter( presenter );
    for( Video movie : mVideos ) {
        if( category.equalsIgnoreCase( movie.getCategory() ) )
            listRowAdapter.add( movie );
    }
    if( listRowAdapter.size() > 0 ) {
        HeaderItem header = new HeaderItem( adapter.size() - 1, category );
        adapter.add( new ListRow( header, listRowAdapter ) );
    }
}
setAdapter(adapter);
```

Creating a Presenter

Even though all of the logic for creating your rows of items for the BrowseFragment is complete, you still need to create the CardPresenter object to compile your app and display the data. CardPresenter will be an extension of the Presenter, which exists within the Leanback Support library. The purpose of the Presenter is to take data and bind it to views, similar to the concept of the adapter in a RecyclerView, but without relying on position. If you have worked with RecyclerViews before, this class should look somewhat familiar.

```
public class CardPresenter extends Presenter {
    static class ViewHolder extends Presenter.ViewHolder {
        private ImageCardView mCardView;

        public ViewHolder(View view) {
            super(view);
            mCardView = (ImageCardView) view;
        }

        public ImageCardView getCardView() {
            return mCardView;
        }

        public void updateCardViewImage( Context context, String link ) {
            Picasso.with(context).load(link)
                .resize(210, 210).centerCrop()
                .into(mCardView.getMainImageView());
        }
    }

    @Override
    public ViewHolder onCreateViewHolder(ViewGroup parent) {
        ImageCardView cardView = new ImageCardView( parent.getContext() );
        cardView.setFocusable( true );
        return new ViewHolder(cardView);
    }

    @Override
    public void onBindViewHolder(Presenter.ViewHolder viewHolder,
    Object item) {
        Video video = (Video) item;
        if ( !TextUtils.isEmpty(video.getPoster()) ) {
            ((ViewHolder) viewHolder).mCardView
                .setTitleText(video.getTitle());
            ((ViewHolder) viewHolder).mCardView
                .setMainImageDimensions( 210, 210 );
            ( (ViewHolder) viewHolder )
```

```
                    .updateCardViewImage( ( (ViewHolder) viewHolder )
                    .getCardView().getContext(), video.getPoster() );
        }
    }

    @Override
    public void onUnbindViewHolder(Presenter.ViewHolder viewHolder) {
    }

    @Override
    public void onViewAttachedToWindow(Presenter.ViewHolder viewHolder) {
    }
}
```

> **Note**   RecyclerViews are still a relatively new addition to Android development.
> If you haven't worked with them before, I highly recommend the book *Android
> Recipes*, 4th edition, by Dave Smith. Also published by Apress, it contains a lot
> of amazing examples for Android development, including a strong section on the
> RecyclerView.

While `Presenter` does most of its work behind the scenes, you can see there's still a bit more customizing that needs to be done. The `Presenter` class requires the use of the `ViewHolder` pattern in order to reuse views when cycling through rows with more than a few items. The `ViewHolder` used previously contains a single `ImageCardView`, which is a view designed specifically for Android TV containing a large image and a pre-styled card of information below that image. In order to load the poster image from the data, which happens to be stored as a URL, you will use the Picasso library by Square to load, resize, and center-crop the image.

With your `ViewHolder` defined, you need to create it in `onCreateViewHolder` and set it to be focusable, which allows it to be highlighted by users. When the `ViewHolder` is created, you can return it for use by the `Presenter`. The final method that you will need to override in the `Presenter` is `onBindViewHolder`. As the name implies, this is where you will bind data to the views in the `ViewHolder` so that the `CardPresenter` is displayed correctly.

At this point you should be able to compile and run your application on an Android TV device or emulator. You should see rows representing the data items from `videos.json`, as well as the category headers for each group of videos, as shown in Figure 3-2. While there's some more customization that can be done to the `BrowseFragment`, we'll save that for the next chapter in this book.

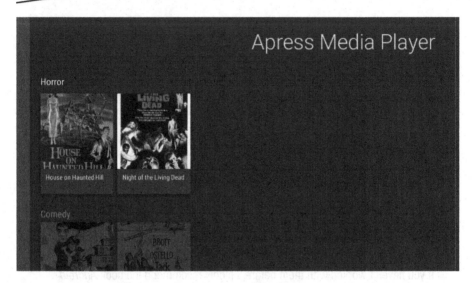

Figure 3-2. BrowseFragment with cards for each piece of media

Creating a Video Details Screen

While the BrowseFragment is designed to give your users a quick glimpse of what they have available to enjoy, the DetailsFragment is meant to focus on one item. This detail screen not only gives the user more information about the content, but also allows them to perform various actions and view related content.

Setting Up Video Details

You can start building out your details screen by creating a new Java file in your media player package and naming it VideoDetailsActivity. Like MainActivity, VideoDetailsActivity will simply set a layout for the content view that contains a fragment.

```
public class VideoDetailsActivity extends Activity {
    @Override
    public void onCreate(Bundle savedInstanceState)
    {
        super.onCreate(savedInstanceState);
        setContentView(R.layout.activity_video_details);
    }
}
```

You will also need to create the layout file that is being used. Go into the res/layout directory and create a new XML file named activity_ video_details. This layout will only contain a fragment named VideoDetailsFragment.

```xml
<?xml version="1.0" encoding="utf-8"?>
<fragment xmlns:android="http://schemas.android.com/apk/res/android"
    xmlns:tools="http://schemas.android.com/tools"
    android:id="@+id/video_detail_fragment"
    android:name="com.apress.mediaplayer.VideoDetailsFragment"
    android:layout_width="match_parent"
    android:layout_height="match_parent"
    tools:deviceIds="tv"
    tools:ignore="MergeRootFrame" />
```

Now that you have an activity with a layout, you will need to create the VideoDetailsFragment in your Java application package directory. When the file is created, have it extend DetailsFragment and implement the OnItemViewClickedListener and OnActionClickedListener interfaces. OnItemViewClickedListener is similar to a standard OnItemClickedListener, except that it is a part of the Leanback Support library and designed specifically as a callback for when an item in a row view holder is clicked. OnActionClickedListener, as the name implies, is called when an action item is clicked. You will need to override the OnItemClicked and onActionClicked methods for the interfaces.

```java
public class VideoDetailsFragment extends DetailsFragment
        implements OnItemViewClickedListener, OnActionClickedListener {

    @Override
    public void onItemClicked(Presenter.ViewHolder itemViewHolder,
                              Object item,
                              RowPresenter.ViewHolder rowViewHolder,
                              Row row) {

    }

    @Override
    public void onActionClicked(Action action) {
    }
}
```

Wiring Up Video Details

Now that you have the base DetailsFragment built, you will need to add a static string to the top of the class that will be used for passing a serialized Video object to the fragment.

```
public static final String EXTRA_VIDEO = "extra_video";
```

Next you'll need to tie in the BrowseFragment to the DetailsFragment. Go back into MainFragment.java and update the class definition line so that MainFragment also implements OnItemViewClickedListener. When a CardPresenter item is clicked, OnItemClicked will be called. You will need to check the data item type associated with the view to see if it is a Video object, and if it is, pass it to the VideoDetailsActivity as an extra when starting the new activity.

```
@Override
public void onItemClicked(Presenter.ViewHolder itemViewHolder,
                          Object item,
                          RowPresenter.ViewHolder rowViewHolder,
                          Row row) {
    if( item instanceof Video ) {
        Video video = (Video) item;
        Intent intent = new Intent( getActivity(),
        VideoDetailActivity.class );
        intent.putExtra( VideoDetailsFragment.EXTRA_VIDEO, video );
        startActivity( intent );
    }
}
```

When your onItemClick method is defined, you will need to associate it with MainFragment so that the app knows to call onItemClicked when an item is clicked. You can do this by adding the following line as the last item in onActivityCreated.

```
setOnItemViewClickedListener( this );
```

Finally, you need to register VideoDetailsActivity in AndroidManifest.xml so that it can be launched.

```
<activity android:name=".VideoDetailsActivity" />
```

At this point you should be able to run your application. If everything went as expected, you will be able to click on one of the items in BrowseFragment to open up the VideoDetailsActivity, though VideoDetailsFragment should only display a blank screen.

Displaying Content Details

The main component of the DetailsFragment is the DetailsOverviewRow. DetailsOverviewRow consists of a main image, a text view for displaying a description, and an optional series of action buttons. Before you populate your DetailsOverviewRow with information, you should declare four member variables at the top of the VideoDetailsFragment class.

```java
public static final long ACTION_WATCH = 1;
private Video mVideo;
private DetailsOverviewRow mRow;
private Target target = new Target() {
    @Override
    public void onBitmapLoaded(Bitmap bitmap, Picasso.LoadedFrom from) {
        mRow.setImageBitmap(getActivity(), bitmap);
    }

    @Override
    public void onBitmapFailed(Drawable errorDrawable) {
    }

    @Override
    public void onPrepareLoad(Drawable placeHolderDrawable) {
    }
};
```

ACTION_WATCH is an identifier that will be used when the user selects to view the content. mVideo is the data object that you will use for displaying content. mRow is simply a reference to the DetailsOverviewRow so that it can be accessed easily. Finally, Target is a part of the Picasso library and allows you to load remote images into it so that your program can use them without being loaded directly into an ImageView. In the case of the DetailsFragment, images will be loaded into the Target and sent to onBitmapLoaded, which will then call setImageBitmap on the DetailsOverviewRow.

The onCreate method is where you handle the logic behind VideoDetailsFragment. The first thing you will do is retrieve the content data from the intent used to start the details activity, then you can initialize mRow as a new DetailsOverviewRow.

```java
@Override
public void onCreate(Bundle savedInstanceState) {
    super.onCreate(savedInstanceState);
    mVideo = (Video) getActivity().getIntent().getSerializableExtra( EXTRA_
    VIDEO );
    mRow = new DetailsOverviewRow( mVideo );
}
```

Next you can create the actions that will be available for the user to select. If you looked over the Hello World example in Chapter 1, you'll notice that the addAction method is used by the sample, but struck through by Android Studio because it is deprecated. The currently accepted way to add actions to the DetailsOverviewRow is to pass a SparseArrayObjectAdapter through the setActionsAdapter method. SparseArrayObjectAdapter has two methods that you will need to override: size and get. size returns the number of action buttons that you want to display, and get handles returning a new action to display. For this example, we will use a size of 3, though only the first item will perform a real action. Create a new method called initAction as defined here and invoke it from onCreate.

```java
private void initActions() {
    mRow.setActionsAdapter(new SparseArrayObjectAdapter() {
        @Override
        public int size() {
            return 3;
        }

        @Override
        public Object get(int position) {
            if(position == 0) {
                return new Action(ACTION_WATCH, "Watch", "");
            } else if( position == 1 ) {
                return new Action( 42, "Rent", "Line 2" );
            } else if( position == 2 ) {
                return new Action( 42, "Preview", "" );
            }

            else return null;
        }
    });
}
```

With your actions defined, it's time to start creating the presenter that will be used for the details fragment. Below the call to initActions in onCreate, you will create a ClassPresenterSelector and an ArrayObjectAdapter then add the DetailsOverviewRow to the ArrayObjectAdapter.

```java
ClassPresenterSelector presenterSelector = createDetailsPresenter();
ArrayObjectAdapter adapter = new ArrayObjectAdapter( presenterSelector );
adapter.add(mRow);
```

Here createDetailsPresenter is a helper method that returns a
ClassPresenterSelector. You will create this helper method now. In the Hello
World sample application, DetailsOverviewRowPresenter is used, but also
deprecated. Instead you will use a FullWidthDetailsOverviewRowPresenter,
which consists of a logo on the left, a row of actions on the top, and a
customizable detail description view on the right. This presenter lets you
customize the background color of the fragment and action buttons, set
animations, associate an action listener, and add other customizations
to delight your users. When your presenter is built, bind it to the
DetailsOverviewRow and add it to the ClassPresenterSelector. You will also
want to add an empty ListRowPresenter to the ClassPresenterSelector that
will be used to display related media before returning it.

```
private ClassPresenterSelector createDetailsPresenter() {
    ClassPresenterSelector presenterSelector = new ClassPresenterSelector();
    FullWidthDetailsOverviewRowPresenter presenter =
            new FullWidthDetailsOverviewRowPresenter(
                new DetailsDescriptionPresenter() );
    presenter.setOnActionClickedListener(this);
    presenterSelector.addClassPresenter(DetailsOverviewRow.class,
                                        presenter);
    presenterSelector.addClassPresenter(ListRow.class,
                                        new ListRowPresenter());

    return presenterSelector;
}
```

By now you should notice that the DetailsDescriptionPresenter used
by FullWidthDetailsOverviewRowPresenter is not a class provided by the
Leanback Support library. This is a class that you will need to create, so go
ahead and do that now under your app package in the java directory. The
class should be an extension of AbstractDetailsDescriptionPresenter and
will override the onBindDescription method in order to set all of the text for
the detail section of your fragment.

```
public class DetailsDescriptionPresenter extends
    AbstractDetailsDescriptionPresenter {
@Override
protected void onBindDescription(
    AbstractDetailsDescriptionPresenter.ViewHolder viewHolder, Object item) {
        Video video = (Video) item;
        if (video != null) {
            viewHolder.getTitle().setText(video.getTitle());
            viewHolder.getSubtitle().setText(video.getCategory());
            viewHolder.getBody().setText(video.getDescription());
        }
    }
}
```

When your presenters are built, go to the end of onCreate and add the following two lines

```
loadRelatedMedia(adapter);
setAdapter(adapter);
```

At this point you should be able to run your application and get to the video details screen, as seen in Figure 3-3.

Figure 3-3. FullWidthDetailsOverviewRowPresenter with actions and data

loadRelatedMedia is another helper method that you will create, and it will be used for finding and displaying content related to the currently displayed detail screen. setAdapter will bind everything together with the DetailsFragment so that it can be displayed for your users.

The loadRelatedMedia method is where you access a backend or perform any other logic for your app in order to show related content. For this example you will simply load in all of the data from videos.json and display items that are in the same category as the selected video. You will access videos.json in the same fashion as BrowseFragment, using reflection and GSON to create a list of video objects. Once you have your data, you will create an ArrayObjectAdapter and add related video objects to it. Finally you will add the adapter with a header as a ListRow to the DetailsFragment.

```
private void loadRelatedMedia( ArrayObjectAdapter adapter ) {
    String json = Utils.loadJSONFromResource( getActivity(), R.raw.videos );
    Gson gson = new Gson();
    Type collection = new TypeToken<ArrayList<Video>>(){}.getType();
    List<Video> videos = gson.fromJson( json, collection );
    if( videos == null )
        return;

    ArrayObjectAdapter listRowAdapter =
        new ArrayObjectAdapter( new CardPresenter() );

    for( Video video : videos ) {
        if( video.getCategory().equals( mVideo.getCategory() )
            && !video.getTitle().equals( mVideo.getTitle() ) ) {
            listRowAdapter.add( video );
        }
    }

    HeaderItem header = new HeaderItem( 0, "Related" );
    adapter.add(new ListRow(header, listRowAdapter));
}
```

Back in onCreate, add two more lines to the end of the method. The first is a call to Picasso to load the poster for the currently selected video content into the Target object defined at the top of the class with a set size. The second line associates the OnItemViewClickedListener interface with the DetailsFragment, which will allow your row of related content to be clickable by the users.

```
Picasso.with(getActivity()).load(mVideo.getPoster())
        .resize(274, 274).into(target);
setOnItemViewClickedListener(this);
```

At this point you should be able to run your application and select a video on the BrowseFragment to be taken to a functioning DetailsFragment screen. You should see a movie poster, the action buttons, and a text description for the content. If you scroll down there should also be at least one related item that is selectable (see Figure 3-4). You can fix that now by updating the onItemClicked method so that it opens a new VideoDetailsFragment with the information from the related video.

```
@Override
public void onItemClicked(Presenter.ViewHolder itemViewHolder, Object item,

                        RowPresenter.ViewHolder mRowViewHolder, Row mRow) {
    if( item instanceof Video ) {
        Video video = (Video) item;
        Intent intent = new Intent( getActivity(),
```

```
                    VideoDetailActivity.class );
        intent.putExtra( VideoDetailsFragment.EXTRA_VIDEO, video );
        startActivity( intent );
    }
}
```

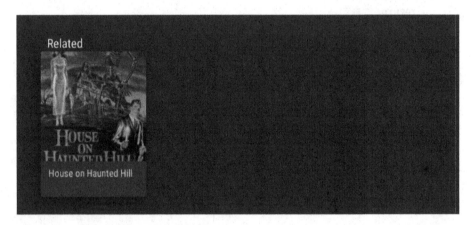

Figure 3-4. Related media on the detail screen

Finally, you need to handle the action buttons at the top of the fragment. If one of the buttons is clicked, onActionClicked will be called. When the Watch button is clicked, you will want to start playing content for your users. The other two actions are used in this sample for emphasis, so you can simply display a Toast message when one is clicked.

```
@Override
public void onActionClicked(Action action) {
    if( action.getId() == ACTION_WATCH ) {
        Intent intent = new Intent(getActivity(),
            PlayerActivity.class);
        intent.putExtra(VideoDetailsFragment.EXTRA_VIDEO,
            mVideo);
        startActivity(intent);
    } else {
        Toast.makeText( getActivity(), "Action",
            Toast.LENGTH_SHORT ).show();
    }
}
```

At this point PlayerActivity does not exist, so the project will not compile. In the next section you will create PlayerActivity to play a video and use the Leanback Support library to add controls to the screen.

Playing and Controlling Content

Without a doubt, playing content is the most important part of a media application. How you play back your content will depend on the type of media you are using for your user, whether you're using a proprietary content player, if the media is local or remote, and if you have other requirements such as DRM or advertisements. In order to keep this example simple, you will create an activity with a VideoView for playing back the video. You will also use a new PlaybackOverlayFragment from the Leanback Support library to display media controls for your users.

Creating the Media Player

You should start by creating a new Activity called PlayerActivity in the same location as your other Java source files. You will also want to add PlayerActivity to AndroidManifest.xml, just like you did with VideoDetailsActivity. Once you have PlayerActivity created and registered in the manifest, you can start fleshing it out.

There will be two member variables at the top of the class, one representing the VideoView that will play the content, and a Video object storing the media data. You will also need to override onCreate and associate a layout with PlayerActivity.

```
public class PlayerActivity extends Activity {
    private VideoView mVideoView;
    private Video mVideo;

    @Override
    public void onCreate(Bundle savedInstanceState) {
        super.onCreate(savedInstanceState);
        setContentView(R.layout.activity_player);
    }
}
```

Next, you will need to create the activity_player.xml layout file. Under xml/layouts, create a new Android layout file and name it activity_player. The layout will consist of two main parts: the VideoView and a new fragment called PlayerControlsFragment that you will write soon.

```
<?xml version="1.0" encoding="utf-8"?>
<RelativeLayout
    xmlns:android="http://schemas.android.com/apk/res/android"
    android:layout_width="match_parent"
    android:layout_height="match_parent"
    android:background="@android:color/black">
```

```
<VideoView
    android:id="@+id/video_view"
    android:layout_width="match_parent"
    android:layout_height="match_parent"
    android:layout_centerInParent="true" />

<fragment
    android:id="@+id/player_controls"
    android:layout_width="match_parent"
    android:layout_height="match_parent"
    android:name="com.apress.mediaplayer.PlayerControlsFragment" />
</RelativeLayout>
```

Back in PlayerActivity, at the end of onCreate, you will need to retrieve the VideoView and data. Once you have both member variables initialized, you can call setVideoPath on the VideoView to set the Video object's URL as the media source.

```
mVideoView = (VideoView) findViewById( R.id.video_view );
mVideo = (Video) getIntent().getSerializableExtra( VideoDetailsFragment.
EXTRA_VIDEO );
mVideoView.setVideoPath( mVideo.getVideoUrl() );
```

Building the Playback Control Fragment

In order to compile your app, you will need to make PlayerControlsFragment. Create a new Java class under your package directory named PlayerControlsFragment and have it extend PlaybackOverlayFragment. PlaybackOverlayFragment contains an ObjectAdapter that vertically stacks rows of action buttons, making it a convenient way to display controls over your content for your user to interact with. You will also need to implement OnActionClickedListener, which will receive a call when a control action is clicked.

```
public class PlayerControlsFragment extends PlaybackOverlayFragment
implements OnActionClickedListener {
    public void onActionClicked(Action action) {
    }
}
```

You will also need to create a new interface inside of PlayerControlsFragment to link the fragment with PlayerActivity. This is how you manipulate the video content from the controls. To keep things simple, you will only add a start and stop method to the interface.

```
public interface PlayerControlsListener {
    void play();
    void pause();
}
```

Now you will need to implement this interface in PlayerActivity. Go back to PlayerActivity and update the class definition to use PlayerControlsListener.

```
public class PlayerActivity extends Activity implements
    PlayerControlsFragment.PlayerControlsListener
```

You will then need to override the two methods in the interface for starting and pausing the VideoView.

```
@Override
public void play() {
    mVideoView.start();
}
```

```
@Override
public void pause() {
    mVideoView.pause();
}
```

With the interface set up on PlayerActivity, you can close it and focus on PlayerControlsFragment. Start by adding two member variables to the top, one for the Video object and another for the interface.

```
private PlayerControlsListener mControlsCallback;
private Video mVideo;
```

Then override onCreate and initialize both member variables. This is also where you can set some basic properties for the PlaybackOverlayFragment. For this project you will set a light translucent background for the controls and disable fading so that the controls stay on the screen until you re-enable fading.

```
@Override
public void onCreate(Bundle savedInstanceState) {
    super.onCreate(savedInstanceState);
    setBackgroundType(PlaybackOverlayFragment.BG_LIGHT);
    setFadingEnabled(false);

    mControlsCallback = (PlayerControlsListener) getActivity();
    mVideo = (Video) getActivity().getIntent()
            .getSerializableExtra(VideoDetailsFragment.EXTRA_VIDEO);
}
```

The remaining portions of the playback controls can be broken into smaller methods. Include the following member variables at the top of the class.

```
private ArrayObjectAdapter mRowsAdapter;
private ArrayObjectAdapter mPrimaryActionsAdapter;
private ArrayObjectAdapter mSecondaryActionsAdapter;
private PlaybackControlsRow mPlaybackControlsRow;

private PlaybackControlsRow.PlayPauseAction mPlayPauseAction;
private PlaybackControlsRow.RepeatAction mRepeatAction;
private PlaybackControlsRow.ShuffleAction mShuffleAction;
private PlaybackControlsRow.FastForwardAction mFastForwardAction;
private PlaybackControlsRow.RewindAction mRewindAction;
private PlaybackControlsRow.SkipNextAction mSkipNextAction;
private PlaybackControlsRow.SkipPreviousAction mSkipPreviousAction;
private PlaybackControlsRow.HighQualityAction mHighQualityAction;
private PlaybackControlsRow.ClosedCaptioningAction mClosedCaptionAction;
```

mRowsAdapter will be used to vertically display horizontal rows of action buttons and other details for the controls. mPlaybackControlsRow, mPrimaryActionsAdapter, and mSecondaryActionsAdapter contain additional details for the controls and actions that can be taken by the users. The remaining items each represent a different predefined action that can be displayed on the PlaybackOverlayFragment.

Next you will add a new method call to the end of onCreate named setupPlaybackControlsRow. This method will initialize the three instances of ArrayObjectAdapter and assign a ControlButtonPresenterSelector that determines what buttons should be displayed at any given time.

```
private void setupPlaybackControlsRow() {
    mPlaybackControlsRow = new PlaybackControlsRow( mVideo );
    ControlButtonPresenterSelector presenterSelector =
            new ControlButtonPresenterSelector();
    mPrimaryActionsAdapter = new ArrayObjectAdapter(presenterSelector);
    mSecondaryActionsAdapter = new ArrayObjectAdapter(presenterSelector);
    mPlaybackControlsRow.setPrimaryActionsAdapter(mPrimaryActionsAdapter);
    mPlaybackControlsRow.setSecondaryActionsAdapter(
            mSecondaryActionsAdapter);
}
```

After setupPlaybackControlsRow is written, add a call to setupPresenter to onCreate. setupPresenter will associate the OnActionClickedListener with the fragment, create the class presenter, and add the PlaybackControlsRow to main adapter for PlayerControlsFragment.

```
private void setupPresenter() {
    ClassPresenterSelector ps = new ClassPresenterSelector();
    PlaybackControlsRowPresenter playbackControlsRowPresenter =
            new PlaybackControlsRowPresenter( new DescriptionPresenter() );
    playbackControlsRowPresenter.setOnActionClickedListener(this);
    playbackControlsRowPresenter.setSecondaryActionsHidden(false);
    ps.addClassPresenter(PlaybackControlsRow.class,
            playbackControlsRowPresenter);
    ps.addClassPresenter(ListRow.class, new ListRowPresenter());
    mRowsAdapter = new ArrayObjectAdapter(ps);
    mRowsAdapter.add(mPlaybackControlsRow);
}
```

You'll notice that DescriptionPresenter is passed into the constructor for PlaybackControlsRowPresenter. DescriptionPresenter extends AbstractDetailsDescriptionPresenter and is an inner class for PlayerControlsFragment. It is used for adding details above the controls. In this case it will add the name of the media above the controls. If you instead pass null into the constructor for PlaybackControlsRowPresenter, you will only see the controls on the overlay.

```
static class DescriptionPresenter extends
AbstractDetailsDescriptionPresenter {
    @Override
    protected void onBindDescription(ViewHolder viewHolder, Object item) {
        viewHolder.getTitle().setText(((Video) item).getTitle());
    }
}
```

Creating Actions

Now that your rows are initialized, it's time to add action buttons to them. Place the following four method calls to the end of onCreate.

```
initActions();
setupPrimaryActionsRow();
setupSecondaryActionsRow();
setAdapter(mRowsAdapter);
```

initActions will initialize each of the member variable actions as new objects. Each action will appear as a button on the controls overlay.

```
private void initActions() {
    mPlayPauseAction =
        new PlaybackControlsRow.PlayPauseAction(getActivity());
    mRepeatAction =
        new PlaybackControlsRow.RepeatAction(getActivity());
```

```
mShuffleAction =
    new PlaybackControlsRow.ShuffleAction(getActivity());
mSkipNextAction =
    new PlaybackControlsRow.SkipNextAction(getActivity());
mSkipPreviousAction =
    new PlaybackControlsRow.SkipPreviousAction(getActivity());
mFastForwardAction =
    new PlaybackControlsRow.FastForwardAction(getActivity());
mRewindAction =
    new PlaybackControlsRow.RewindAction(getActivity());
mHighQualityAction =
    new PlaybackControlsRow.HighQualityAction(getActivity());
mClosedCaptionAction =
    new PlaybackControlsRow.ClosedCaptioningAction(getActivity());
}
```

You can specify which row each action goes into by assigning them to the proper adapter. setupPrimaryActionsRow will add the skip back, rewind, play/pause, fast forward, and skip forward to the top control row. setupSecondaryActionsRow will add the repeat, shuffle, high quality toggle, and closed caption options to the bottom row. It should be noted that the order in which you assign actions to an adapter is directly related to the order that they are displayed from left to right.

```
private void setupPrimaryActionsRow() {
    mPrimaryActionsAdapter.add(mSkipPreviousAction);
    mPrimaryActionsAdapter.add(mRewindAction);
    mPrimaryActionsAdapter.add(mPlayPauseAction);
    mPrimaryActionsAdapter.add(mFastForwardAction);
    mPrimaryActionsAdapter.add(mSkipNextAction);
}

private void setupSecondaryActionsRow() {
    mSecondaryActionsAdapter.add(mRepeatAction);
    mSecondaryActionsAdapter.add(mShuffleAction);
    mSecondaryActionsAdapter.add(mHighQualityAction);
    mSecondaryActionsAdapter.add(mClosedCaptionAction);
}
```

At this point you can run the application and launch the video player activity to see the playback controls as shown in Figure 3-5.

Figure 3-5. Video playback controls

You'll notice that the video does not automatically start, and the buttons don't do anything. While the onActionClicked method has been associated with the controls, the method itself doesn't do anything yet. You can take care of that now.

```
@Override
public void onActionClicked(Action action) {
    if(action.getId() == mPlayPauseAction.getId()) {
        if(mPlayPauseAction.getIndex()
                == PlaybackControlsRow.PlayPauseAction.PLAY) {
            setFadingEnabled(true);
            mControlsCallback.play();
            mRowsAdapter.notifyArrayItemRangeChanged(0, 1);
        } else {
            setFadingEnabled( false );
            mControlsCallback.pause();
        }
        ((PlaybackControlsRow.MultiAction) action).nextIndex();
        mPrimaryActionsAdapter.notifyArrayItemRangeChanged(
                mPrimaryActionsAdapter.indexOf(action), 1);
    } else {
        Toast.makeText( getActivity(), "Other action",
                Toast.LENGTH_SHORT ).show();
    }
}
```

If the clicked action is the Play/Pause button, you will check the state of the button. If the button is in the Play state, you will enable control fading so that the controls disappear from the screen and notify PlayerActivity that it should start playing the video. If the clicked button is Pause, control fading will be disabled so that the controls stay visible, and PlayerActivity will be notified that the media should be paused. The final thing you have to handle when the Play/Pause button is pressed is changing the button state.

Since the PlayPauseAction is an extension of the MultiAction class, you can call notifyArrayItemRangeChanged on the primary row of actions and it will handle changing the button type. If any other button is pressed, this sample will display a Toast message. If you want to change this, you can control what happens in your app for any button by checking the ID against the predefined actions.

Summary

Congratulations! You've made the basis for a full working media application. Now you should be able to run the application and view all of the media in the BrowseFragment, enter into the DetailsFragment to see more information about each piece of content, and control the video using the controls provided by the Leanback Support library. While this is a great first step, there's still plenty more that can be done to customize your app. In the next chapter you will learn how to enhance your app by implementing a local search component, preferences, and adding searching and recommendations to the Android TV home screen. You will also be introduced to additional components that are useful for Android TV development, but don't necessarily fit into the scope of this demo application.

Chapter 4

Enriching Your Media Apps

While the application that you built in the last chapter is a nice demonstration of how to create a bare-bones media app, you will undoubtedly want to add more features for your users. Luckily, the Android TV platform and Leanback Support library offer multiple tools that you can use to improve your app and engage with your users. In this chapter you will learn how to implement simple versions of global and local search, adding a preferences screen to your app and supplying recommendations to the Android TV home screen recommendations row by updating the demo app you created in the last chapter. You will also learn about additional features that are available for Android TV, such as live channels and the Now Playing card.

In-App Searching

When you have an application with a lot of content, it becomes important that your users can find specific media items that they are looking for. Luckily, the BrowseFragment class supports a new built-in view called the SearchOrbView. When the users click on the SearchOrbView, they should be shown a new fragment that facilitates searching within your app. In this section you learn how to add SearchOrbView to MainFragment and use local search within the demonstration application that you started in the last chapter.

Adding a SearchOrbView

Since BrowseFragment contains a built-in SearchOrbView, you can easily make it accessible with a few lines of code. In MainFragment, add a new method call at the end of onActivityCreated named initSearchOrb, so that onActivityCreated looks like the following

```
@Override
public void onActivityCreated(Bundle savedInstanceState) {
    super.onActivityCreated(savedInstanceState);
    loadData();

    setTitle("Apress Media Player");
    setHeadersState(HEADERS_HIDDEN);
    setHeadersTransitionOnBackEnabled(true);
    loadRows();
    setOnItemViewClickedListener( this );
    initSearchOrb();
}
```

Before you initialize the search, go into app/src/res/values and create a new values resource file named colors.xml. This file will contain a few colors that you will use throughout your app in one easy to access location. When the file is created, add a new color named search_button_color and give it any color hex value that fits the theme of your application. This example uses an orange, as defined by #FFA500. Your colors.xml file should look like this:

```
<?xml version="1.0" encoding="utf-8"?>
<resources>
    <color name="search_button_color">#FFA500</color>
</resources>
```

Next you will need to define the initSearchOrb method in your MainFragment class. This method will be where you can set the SearchOrbView color and determine what it does when clicked. In order to make the SearchOrbView visible, the only thing you need to do is set an OnClickListener through the setOnSearchClickedListener method. You will also set the color of the SearchOrbView to the color defined by search_button_color in colors.xml by calling setSearchAffordanceColor.

```
private void initSearchOrb() {

    setSearchAffordanceColor(ContextCompat.getColor(getActivity(),
        R.color.search_button_color));
    setOnSearchClickedListener(new View.OnClickListener() {
        @Override
```

```
    public void onClick(View view) {
    }
});
}
```

> **Note**   You may notice that the color here is being retrieved by calling
> ContextCompat.getColor. Using getResources().getColor(int
> colorResource) has been deprecated as of SDK 23, and this is the
> recommended way of retrieving a color from a resource.

When you run your application, you should now see the search orb in the
top-left corner of your BrowseFragment, as shown in Figure 4-1. You will
notice that the SearchOrbView has some animations already built into it
that cause the orb to grow in size when highlighted, and also pulsate with a
ripple effect in order to let the users know that it is selectable.

Figure 4-1. BrowseFragment with a SearchOrbView visible

When you select the SearchOrbView, you'll notice that nothing
happens. That's because the OnClickListener that is associated with
the SearchOrbView is empty. Before you can make SearchOrbView do
something when it's selected, you need to define a new activity and
fragment to handle searching.

Creating the Local Search Activity and Fragment

Within your application package folder, you will need to create two new Java files. Name the first one MediaSearchActivity.java and have it extend Activity. The only thing this activity will do for now is set a content view for a layout file that you will define later in this section.

```
public class MediaSearchActivity extends Activity {
    @Override
    protected void onCreate(Bundle savedInstanceState) {
        super.onCreate(savedInstanceState);
        setContentView( R.layout.activity_search );
    }
}
```

The second Java file should be named MediaSearchFragment.java, and it will extend the Leanback Support library class SearchFragment. SearchFragment will allow you to implement your own SearchResultProvider and return an ObjectAdapter containing the results, which will then be used to render a RowsFragment in the same way as BrowseFragment.

You will also need to implement the SpeechRecognitionCallback interface. SpeechRecognitionCallback was added with the release of Android Marshmallow as a replacement for SpeechRecognizer. This callback is used so that the users do not need to explicitly grant the RECORD_AUDIO permission to use voice actions while performing a search.

Lastly, you will need to implement OnItemViewClickedListener so that you can determine which action to take when a user selects an item that is returned as a search result. Once you have created MediaSearchFragment and added the interfaces with their method stubs, your class should look like this:

```
public class MediaSearchFragment extends SearchFragment implements
    SpeechRecognitionCallback,
    SearchFragment.SearchResultProvider,
    OnItemViewClickedListener {

    @Override
    public void onItemClicked(Presenter.ViewHolder itemViewHolder,
        Object item, RowPresenter.ViewHolder rowViewHolder, Row row) {
    }

    @Override
    public ObjectAdapter getResultsAdapter() {
        return null;
    }
```

```java
@Override
public boolean onQueryTextChange(String newQuery) {
    return false;
}

@Override
public boolean onQueryTextSubmit(String query) {
    return false;
}

@Override
public void recognizeSpeech() {
}
}
```

Now that your two Java files are implemented, you will need to create the layout file that MediaSearchActivity uses in order to display MediaSearchFragment. Under app/src/main/res/layout, create a new layout XML file named activity_search.xml. This file will look similar to activity_main.xml, except that it will contain a reference to the MediaSearchFragment class.

```xml
<?xml version="1.0" encoding="utf-8"?>
<fragment xmlns:android="http://schemas.android.com/apk/res/android"
    xmlns:tools="http://schemas.android.com/tools"
    android:id="@+id/main_browse_fragment"
    android:name="com.apress.mediaplayer.MediaSearchFragment"
    android:layout_width="match_parent"
    android:layout_height="match_parent"
    tools:context=".MainActivity"
    tools:deviceIds="tv"
    tools:ignore="MergeRootFrame" />
```

Next, you will need to declare MediaSearchActivity inside of the manifest file so that you will be able to use it without your application crashing. You can place the following line of code below the definitions for VideoDetailsActivity and PlayerActivity in AndroidManifest.xml.

```xml
<activity android:name=".MediaSearchActivity" />
```

The last thing you need to do before digging into the code that makes searching possible is connect the SearchOrbView to your new MediaSearchActivity. Returning to MainFragment, create an intent that launches your new search screen when the orb is clicked by updating the onClick method inside of the SearchOrbView onClickListener.

```
setOnSearchClickedListener(new View.OnClickListener() {
    @Override
    public void onClick(View view) {
        Intent intent = new Intent(getActivity(),
            MediaSearchActivity.class );
        startActivity( intent );
    }
});
```

Implementing Local Search from a Keyboard

At this point you should be able to run your application and select the SearchOrbView, but when you do you'll notice that the application crashes. If you look at the app logs in Android Studio, you'll see that you received an IllegalStateException that says the RECORD_AUDIO permission is required for search. In the last section I mentioned that you will use SpeechRecognitionCallback to make that permission unnecessary. However, you still have some work to do in order to tell the SearchFragment that you want to use your own callback. Start by overriding the onCreate method in MediaSearchFragment and pointing the SearchResultProvider, SpeechRecognitionCallback, and OnItemClickListener interfaces to the MediaSearchFragment since the fragment implements those interfaces itself.

```
@Override
public void onCreate(Bundle savedInstanceState) {
    super.onCreate(savedInstanceState);
    setSearchResultProvider(this);
    setSpeechRecognitionCallback(this);
    setOnItemViewClickedListener(this);
}
```

Now you should be able to build your application and select the search orb to see the beginnings of the application search screen. At this point the screen will consist of a voice search activation button in the top-left corner and an EditText at the top center for accepting typed input, as seen in Figure 4-2.

Figure 4-2. Initial App SearchFragment

When you try to type into the search field, you should get another application crash. This is because the majority of MediaSearchFragment has yet to be implemented to handle searching. While efficient searching is beyond the scope of this book, you will create a rudimentary version of search that checks against the data in the local JSON file in order to return results. Start by declaring three new member variables at the top of this class:

- An integer that will be used as a request code for speech input in the next session

- An ArrayObjectAdapter for storing and displaying results

- A list of video objects for keeping track of all the data that can be searched

```
public static final int SPEECH_REQUEST_CODE = 42;
private ArrayObjectAdapter mRowsAdapter;
private List<Video> mVideos;
```

At the end of onCreate you will call loadData() and initialize mRowsAdapter with a new ListRowPresenter.

```
loadData();
mRowsAdapter = new ArrayObjectAdapter( new ListRowPresenter() );
```

loadData will take the content JSON data and create a list of video objects, and should look familiar to you since you have implemented this method before in other classes for this project.

```
private void loadData() {
    String json = Utils.loadJSONFromResource(getActivity(), R.raw.videos);
    Type collection = new TypeToken<ArrayList<Video>>(){}.getType();
    Gson gson = new Gson();
    mVideos = gson.fromJson(json, collection);
}
```

Now that you have the data prepared, it's time to start searching. For this example you will use a method named loadQuery that will accept a string from your users and find content from the data that matches the query. This method will first clear the results of previous searches and validate that the query exists and is not empty. Next you will loop through the data and see if the media titles contain the query provided by the users. While this is not the most efficient way to retrieve results from the data, it is a simple and easy-to-understand approach while learning how Android TV displays search results. Each item that matches the search query will be placed into a new ArrayObjectAdapter to be displayed as cards. Once the ArrayObjectAdapter is populated with the results, a new Header and ListRow will be added to the top-level ArrayObjectAdapter to display the results.

```
private void loadQuery(String query) {
    if(mRowsAdapter != null)
        mRowsAdapter.clear();
    if(query == null || query.length() == 0)
        return;

    ArrayObjectAdapter listRowAdapter = new
        ArrayObjectAdapter(new CardPresenter());
    for(Video video : mVideos) {
        if(video.getTitle() != null &&
            video.getTitle().toLowerCase().contains(query.toLowerCase())) {
            listRowAdapter.add(video);
        }
    }

    if(listRowAdapter.size() == 0)
        return;
    HeaderItem header = new HeaderItem("Results");
    mRowsAdapter.add(new ListRow(header, listRowAdapter));
}
```

When loadQuery is complete, you will need to wire it up to
MediaSearchFragment so that the application knows to call that method.
You have three stub methods from the SearchResultProvider interface that
you will need to use. getResultsAdapter will simply return mRowsAdapter so
that the fragment will know what will be displayed. onQueryTextChange and
onQueryTextSubmit will each take the query string argument and then call
loadQuery. You will notice that both of these methods also return a Boolean.
If you return true, it means that the results have changed due to the query.
For this simple demonstration we will always return true, even though the
results may not be different from the last time one of these methods was
called, in order to keep things simple.

```
@Override
public ObjectAdapter getResultsAdapter() {
    return mRowsAdapter;
}

@Override
public boolean onQueryTextChange(String newQuery) {
    loadQuery(newQuery);
    return true;
}

@Override
public boolean onQueryTextSubmit(String query) {
    loadQuery(query);
    return true;
}
```

At this point you will be able to run your application and type in your search
query to return results, as seen in Figure 4-3.

Figure 4-3. In-app search screen implementation

The last thing you will want to do to complete searching through text is perform an action when one of the returned search results is selected. You can do this by overriding the onItemClicked method from the OnItemViewClickedListener interface. When an item is selected, ensure that it is an instance of a video object, and then pass it to VideoDetailActivity through an intent.

```
@Override
public void onItemClicked(Presenter.ViewHolder itemViewHolder, Object item,
RowPresenter.ViewHolder rowViewHolder, Row row) {
    if(item instanceof Video) {
        Video video = (Video) item;
        Intent intent = new Intent(getActivity(),
            VideoDetailsActivity.class);
        intent.putExtra(VideoDetailsFragment.EXTRA_VIDEO, video);
        startActivity(intent);
    }
}
```

Now when you click on a returned result, the detail screen for that video will be displayed (Figure 4-4) and your users will be able to view the media content.

Figure 4-4. Detail screen shown when selecting an item from search

While being able to type in search queries will be beneficial for your users, many users will still want the ability to just say what they're looking for and have it appear on the screen. In the next section you will learn how to accommodate this by accepting voice input from your users so your app can display search results.

Using Voice Input for Local Search

With the scaffolding put together for searching, adding voice support is fairly straightforward. When you implemented the SpeechRecognitionCallback interface in MediaSearchFragment, you added a stub for the method recognizeSpeech. In this method you will call startActivityForResult with the intent received from getRecognizerIntent and the request code that you defined in the last section at the top of MediaSearchFragment.

```
@Override
public void recognizeSpeech() {

    startActivityForResult(getRecognizerIntent(),
        SPEECH_REQUEST_CODE);
}
```

This will trigger onActivityResult to be called in MediaSearchFragment. Here you will check the value of requestCode to make sure it matches SPEECH_REQUEST_CODE and that resultCode matches Activity.RESULT_OK. If both of those are true, then you will call setSearchQuery. The setSearchQuery method will set the text in the search bar and accept two parameters: an intent containing the search query and a Boolean. Setting the Boolean value to true will automatically call onQueryTextSubmit once the voice input has been received.

```
@Override
public void onActivityResult(int requestCode, int resultCode, Intent data) {
    if(requestCode == SPEECH_REQUEST_CODE
            && resultCode == Activity.RESULT_OK) {
        setSearchQuery(data, true);
    }
}
```

At this point everything in MediaSearchFragment should work as expected if the users select the voice button on the search screen. However, if your users select the voice input button on their remote it will bring up the Android TV global search screen. You can change this behavior so that MediaSearchActivity launches by overriding the onSearchRequested method in your MediaSearchActivity and MainActivity files. This method must also return a Boolean value. If true is returned, then it means a search activity has been started. If false is returned if the action has been blocked.

```
@Override
public boolean onSearchRequested() {
    startActivity(new Intent(this, MediaSearchActivity.class));
    return true;
}
```

With those last few changes, the users will now be taken to your custom search screen whenever they press the search button on their remote control while in your app. You should now be able to take what you have learned about local search and implement it into your own Android TV apps to enrich the experience of your users.

Implementing a Preference Screen

When you want to give your users the ability to customize their experience in an Android app, you generally use the PreferenceFragment class. PreferenceFragment allows you to display a list of items that can be manipulated by the users and automatically saves changes to the application's SharedPreferences. Given how useful this component can be, Google has provided the Leanback Preference library, which contains a customized PreferenceFragment called the LeanbackPreferenceFragment. This new class provides the same functionality as the PreferenceFragment while also conforming to television design patterns. In this section you will learn how to implement it into your demo app.

Since this component uses a library that has not already been added to your project, you will need to include it as a dependency in your build.gradle file. At the time of this writing, version 23.1.1 of this library is the latest. Under the dependencies node of build.gradle, add the following line and then sync your project.

```
compile 'com.android.support:preference-leanback-v17:23.1.1'
```

Displaying a Preference Item Entry Point

If you have looked over the Android TV home screen, you'll notice that the last row consists of two settings items (as seen in Figure 4-5). You will follow this pattern in the demo app by providing a new settings item at the bottom of MainFragment that will open to your LeanbackPreferenceFragment.

Figure 4-5. Android home screen and location of settings

To implement this, you will add a new row and header to the ArrayObjectAdapter containing the rows of media cards in MainFragment. You will also create a new presenter so that the settings item will stand out compared to the media cards that you have used before. Go ahead and get started by creating a new Java class named PreferenceCardPresenter and have it extend the Presenter class. You will need to declare three methods in this class: onCreateViewHolder, onBindViewHolder, and onUnbindViewHolder.

```java
public class PreferenceCardPresenter extends Presenter {
    @Override
    public ViewHolder onCreateViewHolder(ViewGroup parent) {
    }

    @Override
    public void onBindViewHolder(ViewHolder viewHolder, Object item)    {
    }
```

```
    @Override
    public void onUnbindViewHolder(ViewHolder viewHolder) {
    }
}
```

In onCreateViewHolder, you will create a TextView, set the size of that TextView to match the media cards in MainFragment and apply some other styles to make the card gray with centered white text.

```
@Override
public ViewHolder onCreateViewHolder(ViewGroup parent) {
    TextView view = new TextView(parent.getContext());
    view.setLayoutParams(new ViewGroup.LayoutParams(210, 210));
    view.setFocusable(true);
    view.setBackgroundColor(ContextCompat.getColor(parent.getContext(),
        R.color.preference_card_background));
    view.setTextColor(Color.WHITE);
    view.setGravity(Gravity.CENTER);
    return new ViewHolder(view);
}
```

Next you will need to take the object that was passed to the class, cast it to a string, and use that string to set the text that will be displayed for this item.

```
@Override
public void onBindViewHolder(ViewHolder viewHolder, Object item) {
    ((TextView) viewHolder.view).setText((String) item);
}
```

In the onCreateViewHolder method you set the background color for the settings card using a color resource value. For that to work, you will need to add a color resource named preference_card_background to your colors.xml file. Open the colors.xml file under the app/src/main/res/values directory and add the following line within the resources tags

```
<color name="preference_card_background">#AAAAAA</color>
```

When you're done with PreferenceCardPresenter, you can close that file and open MainFragment. Once you have opened MainFragment, add the following code to the end of loadRows.

```
setupPreferences(adapter);
```

setupPreferences will accept the ArrayObjectAdapter used for displaying the rows of media content so that you can append a row containing your preference item to the bottom of your BrowseFragment. In this method you will create a new HeaderItem and PreferenceCardPresenter, then you will initialize a new ArrayObjectAdapter to contain your settings item. Finally, this method will add a new string to the row with the title of your settings item and add the preference row to your main BrowseFragment set of rows.

```
private void setupPreferences(ArrayObjectAdapter adapter) {
    HeaderItem gridHeader = new HeaderItem(adapter.size(), "Preferences");
    PreferenceCardPresenter presenter = new PreferenceCardPresenter();
    ArrayObjectAdapter gridRowAdapter = new ArrayObjectAdapter(presenter);
    gridRowAdapter.add("Settings");
    adapter.add(new ListRow(gridHeader, gridRowAdapter));
}
```

If you run your application now, you will see a gray card with white text in it at the bottom of MainFragment, as seen in Figure 4-6.

Figure 4-6. LeanbackPreferenceFragment entry point in MainFragment

In order to open your preference screen, modify the OnItemClicked method to check if the selected item is equal to "Settings". If it is, create a new Intent for SettingsActivity.class and call startActivity with that intent.

```
@Override
public void onItemClicked(Presenter.ViewHolder itemViewHolder, Object item,
RowPresenter.ViewHolder rowViewHolder, Row row) {
    if(item instanceof Video) {
        Video movie = (Video) item;
        Intent intent = new Intent(getActivity(),
            VideoDetailActivity.class);
```

```
        intent.putExtra(VideoDetailsFragment.EXTRA_VIDEO, movie);
        startActivity(intent);
    } else if("Settings".equals(item)) {
        Intent intent = new Intent(getActivity(), SettingsActivity.class);
        startActivity(intent);
    }
}
```

Creating the Preference Screen

To compile your app, you will need to create a few new files. Under your application package, make a new Java class and name it SettingsActivity. java. This class will extend Activity, and you will override onCreate so that you can set a layout file as the content view.

```
public class SettingsActivity extends Activity {
    @Override
    protected void onCreate(Bundle savedInstanceState) {
        super.onCreate(savedInstanceState);
        setContentView(R.layout.activity_settings);
    }
}
```

Next you will need to create the layout file. Create a new layout file named activity_settings.xml in the layouts resource folder of your project. This should look familiar to you from the last few activity layout files, though this one will contain a reference to a new class you will write called SettingsFragment.

```
<?xml version="1.0" encoding="utf-8"?>
<fragment xmlns:android="http://schemas.android.com/apk/res/android"
    android:id="@+id/settings_fragment"
    android:name="com.apress.mediaplayer.SettingsFragment"
    android:layout_width="match_parent"
    android:layout_height="match_parent" />
```

With the layout created, you can now make the SettingsFragment Java file inside of your application package directory. This new class will extend LeanbackPreferenceFragment and implement the OnSharedPreferenceChangeListener interface.

```
public class SettingsFragment extends LeanbackPreferenceFragment
        implements OnSharedPreferenceChangeListener {
    @Override
    public void onSharedPreferenceChanged(SharedPreferences
        sharedPreferences, String key) {
    }
```

```
    @Override
    public void onCreatePreferences(Bundle bundle, String s) {
    }
}
```

Next you need to override onPause and onResume so that onSharedPreferenceChangedListener can be registered and unregistered.

```
@Override
public void onResume() {
    super.onResume();
    getPreferenceManager().getSharedPreferences()
        .registerOnSharedPreferenceChangeListener(this);
}

@Override
public void onPause() {
    getPreferenceManager().getSharedPreferences()
        .unregisterOnSharedPreferenceChangeListener(this);
    super.onPause();
}
```

The onSharedPreferenceChanged method will be called whenever the user modifies an item on the preference screen, allowing you to change how your application interacts with your users.

The last thing you will need to do in SettingsFragment is override onCreate so that you can associate an XML file defining your preferences with your fragment.

```
@Override
public void onCreate(Bundle savedInstanceState) {
    super.onCreate(savedInstanceState);
    addPreferencesFromResource(R.xml.preferences);
}
```

Now that you've completed SettingsFragment, you will need to make the preferences.xml file. Create a new resource folder under the res directory called xml. Next, create a new XML resource file and name it preferences. xml. Your preferences file will contain various examples of preferences that can be supported on the Android TV, including checked items, a list of selectable items, an EditText dialog, and an item that cannot be selected unless its parent item is checked. It should be noted that some preferences features, such as including an intent that goes to a web page, are not supported in Android TV.

```
<PreferenceScreen
    xmlns:android="http://schemas.android.com/apk/res/android"
    android:title="Preferences">
    <PreferenceCategory
        android:title="Inline Preference">
        <CheckBoxPreference
            android:key="checkbox_preference"
            android:title="CheckboxPreference"
            android:summary="Checkbox Preference Summary" />
    </PreferenceCategory>
    <PreferenceCategory
        android:title="Dialog Preference">
        <EditTextPreference
            android:key="edittext_preference"
            android:title="Edit Text Preference"
            android:summary="Edit Text Preference Summary"
            android:dialogTitle="Dialog Title Edit Text Preference" />
        <ListPreference
            android:key="list_preference"
            android:title="List Preference"
            android:summary="List Preference Summary"
            android:entries="@array/entries_list_preference"
            android:entryValues="@array/entries_list_preference"
            android:dialogTitle="List Preference Dialog Title" />
    </PreferenceCategory>
    <PreferenceCategory
        android:title="Attributes Title">
        <CheckBoxPreference
            android:key="parent_checkbox_preference"
            android:title="Parent Preference Title"
            android:summary="Parent Preference Summary" />
        <CheckBoxPreference
            android:key="child_checkbox_preference"
            android:dependency="parent_checkbox_preference"
            android:title="Child Preference Title"
            android:summary="Child Preference Summary" />
    </PreferenceCategory>
</PreferenceScreen>
```

In this file, a string array named entries_list_preference is used. Within your values resource directory under the res folder, create a new file named string-array.xml and populate it with a list of items. For this demonstration you will just list the first four planets in the solar system; however, you can use any data that you like.

```xml
<?xml version="1.0" encoding="utf-8"?>
<resources>
    <string-array name="entries_list_preference">
        <item>Mercury</item>
        <item>Venus</item>
        <item>Earth</item>
        <item>Mars</item>
    </string-array>
</resources>
```

In order to run your application and get to the new preferences screen, you will need to configure the preferenceTheme style item to the PreferenceThemeOverlay style in your application theme. You can do this by opening styles.xml from your res/values directory and adding the new item under the AppTheme style.

```xml
<?xml version="1.0" encoding="utf-8"?>
<resources>
    <style name="AppTheme" parent="@style/Theme.Leanback">
        <item name="preferenceTheme">@style/PreferenceThemeOverlay</item>
    </style>
</resources>
```

Finally, open AndroidManifest.xml and define a new activity item for SettingsActivity so that the system knows that the activity is available for use within your app.

```xml
<activity android:name=".SettingsActivity" />
```

At this point you should be able to run your application and select the Settings item from MainFragment, leading you into the preference screen. This page will contain a header and a list of items as defined by preferences.xml, as seen in Figure 4-7.

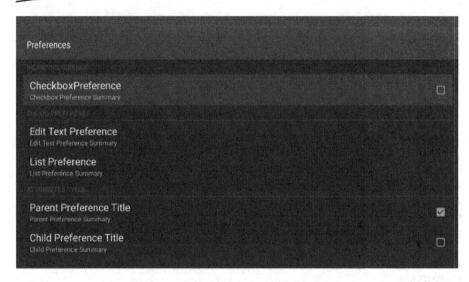

Figure 4-7. LeanbackPreferenceFragment screen

When your users select any item in this fragment, a SharedPreferences entry will be changed to reflect the selection, allowing you to determine how your app should act for your users. Values for check boxes are stored as booleans, the EditText preference saves the content of the EditText field as a string, and the list preference item will present the users with a dialog containing a list of the available options for selecting that will also be stored as a string, as seen in Figure 4-8.

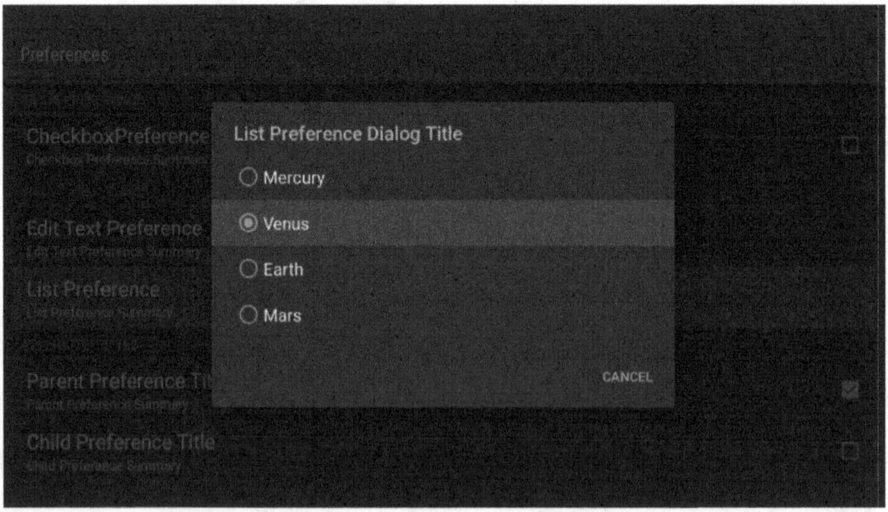

Figure 4-8. LeanbackPreferenceFragment list preference example

In this section you learned about the supported preferences items for Android TV and how to implement them into your application. In the next section you will expand on your demonstration program in order to engage with your users while they are not actively using your app through the use of recommendations that will show up on the Android TV home screen.

Using Recommendations

No matter how nice your app is or how much functionality you build, you have to get users into your app for them to be able to enjoy it. When users are sitting in front of their televisions, they want to be able to find content quickly and start watching. Back in Chapter 2 you were introduced to the recommendations row of the Android TV home screen, and in this section you will learn how to take advantage of this feature to engage with your users.

Building Recommendation Cards

Recommendations are simply notification cards created from a background service that are periodically pushed to the Android TV home screen in order to offer content to your users. You can start pushing out recommendations now by creating a new Java class named RecommendationService under your application's package directory and having it extend IntentService.

```
public class RecommendationService extends IntentService {
    public RecommendationService() {
        super("RecommendationService");
    }

    @Override
    protected void onHandleIntent(Intent intent) {
    }
}
```

There are two member variables that you will need to place at the top of your service for this demonstration: an integer representing the max number of recommendations your app will display for your user, and a list of video objects that you will use to build the recommendations.

```
private int MAX_RECOMMENDATIONS = 3;
private List<Video> mVideos;
```

The onHandleIntent method is where all of the work for creating your recommendations will happen. You can start setting up that method by calling loadData, which will work exactly like it has in other classes, to populate the mVideos structure. Next you will need to create a new

NotificationManager object that will be used for pushing out your set of notification objects once they have been built. When you have your NotificationManager created, you can do some simple contingency planning by checking to see if mVideos is empty or null, and returning if it is. If it is not null or empty, but the number of items in the data is less than the number of recommendations you would normally push out (three in this case), then you can change the number of recommendations so that all of the data you do have will be displayed.

```
@Override
protected void onHandleIntent(Intent intent) {
    loadData();
    NotificationManager notificationManager = (NotificationManager)
     getApplicationContext().getSystemService(Context.NOTIFICATION_SERVICE);

    int numOfRecommendations = MAX_RECOMMENDATIONS;

    if( mVideos == null ) {
        return;
    } else if(mVideos.size() < MAX_RECOMMENDATIONS){
        numOfRecommendations = mVideos.size();
    }
}
```

Because all of the notifications to be built will share some common attributes, you can create a base NotificationCompat.Builder object with the common attributes to be shared across each recommendation.

```
NotificationCompat.Builder builder = new
    NotificationCompat.Builder(getApplicationContext())
        .setSmallIcon(R.mipmap.ic_launcher)
        .setLocalOnly(true)
        .setOngoing(true)

        .setColor(ContextCompat.getColor(getApplicationContext(),
            android.R.color.black))
        .setCategory(Notification.CATEGORY_RECOMMENDATION);
```

This builder will create a notification that:

- Uses the app icon in the lower-right corner of the card
- Will only be relevant to the local device
- Is flagged as ongoing, meaning it has higher priority than notifications that are not ongoing

- Will have a black selected color (though you can use any color that fits the theme of your application)

- Will be categorized as a recommendation by the Android TV home screen

You can finish up the onHandleIntent method by creating a loop to cycle through your data and create the three notifications that you will display, followed by posting them to the NotificationManager. For this example you will simply grab the first three videos from the data set to display, though your own applications will use logic that makes sense for your purposes.

```
for(int i = 0; i < numOfRecommendations; i++ ) {
    Video video = mVideos.get(i);
    Bitmap bitmap;
    try {
            bitmap = Picasso.with(this)
                .load(video.getPoster()).
                resize(313, 176)
                .get();
    } catch( IOException e ) {
        continue;
    }
    builder.setPriority(numOfRecommendations - i)
            .setContentTitle(video.getTitle())
            .setContentText(video.getCategory())
            .setLargeIcon(bitmap)
            .setContentIntent(buildPendingIntent(video, i + 1));

    notificationManager.notify(i + 1, builder.build());
}
```

While you used Picasso in the last chapter to display images on media cards inside of the app, it should be reiterated that Picasso is a third-party open source library from Square, and not a part of the Android framework or official libraries. The call to the Picasso image loader class will synchronously download the image at the URL stored in video.getPoster and resize it to 313 pixels in width by 176 pixels in height. While this width and height may seem arbitrary, they are the dimensions used by Google's own applications, such as the YouTube app, in order to conform to a 16:9 display ratio. This bitmap will then be used as the main image for the recommendation card.

Once your card image has been downloaded, you can set additional properties on the NotificationCompat.Builder object, such as the order in which the recommendations will appear in the recommendations row, the title and description on the card, and the intent that will be fired when the recommendation is selected.

At this point you may notice that your application does not compile. This is because the buildPendingIntent has not yet been defined. This can be remedied by adding the following method within your RecommendationService class.

```
private PendingIntent buildPendingIntent(Video video, long id ) {
    Intent detailsIntent = new Intent(this, VideoDetailActivity.class);
    detailsIntent.putExtra(VideoDetailsFragment.EXTRA_VIDEO, video);

    TaskStackBuilder stackBuilder = TaskStackBuilder.create(this);
    stackBuilder.addParentStack(VideoDetailActivity.class);
    stackBuilder.addNextIntent(detailsIntent);

    detailsIntent.setAction(Long.toString(id));

    PendingIntent intent = stackBuilder.getPendingIntent(0,
        PendingIntent.FLAG_UPDATE_CURRENT);
    return intent;
}
```

This method will create an intent that launches VideoDetailsActivity and associates it with a TaskStackBuilder so that using the back button on the Android TV remote will properly return the users to the Android TV home screen rather than attempting to place them within your app. You will notice that the intent also has a call to setAction. This allows you to ensure that each PendingIntent used for recommendations is unique to the data that created it. Otherwise, each of your recommendations may end up opening to a screen based on the same data, rather than what the users wanted to see. At this point your service will be able to create notifications based on your data and display them as recommendations on the Android TV home screen. In the next section you will learn how to start up this service so that it will automatically start pushing content for your users to enjoy.

Starting the Recommendation Service

The easiest way to start your recommendation service is when your application has been opened by your users. You can do this simply enough by going into MainActivity and adding the following line to the end of onCreate.

```
startService(new Intent(this, RecommendationService.class));
```

Where this strategy runs into trouble is when your users restart their Android TV devices, but have not opened your application. In order to handle this case, your best bet is to create a BroadcastReceiver that listens for when the Android TV device has finished booting up. When the Android TV has started, this BroadcastReceiver will start RecommendationService. To demonstrate this, create a new Java class named BootupReceiver and have it extend BroadcastReceiver.

```
public class BootupReceiver extends BroadcastReceiver {
    @Override
    public void onReceive(Context context, Intent intent) {
    }
}
```

When onReceive is triggered, you will want to check the intent that has been passed to it to see if it is an Intent.ACTION_BOOT_COMPLETED action. If it is, then you can start RecommendationService. You will also want to create a new method named scheduleRecommendationUpdate that creates an AlarmManager in order to restart or update RecommendationService every 30 minutes. This will provide the users with new or updated content from your app in order to hopefully catch their attention and get them into your application.

```
private static final long INITIAL_DELAY = 5000;

@Override
public void onReceive(Context context, Intent intent) {
    if(intent.getAction().endsWith(Intent.ACTION_BOOT_COMPLETED)) {
        context.startService(new Intent(context,
            RecommendationService.class));
        scheduleRecommendationUpdate(context);
    }
}

private void scheduleRecommendationUpdate(Context context) {
    AlarmManager alarmManager = (AlarmManager)
        context.getSystemService(Context.ALARM_SERVICE);
    Intent recommendationIntent = new Intent(context,
        RecommendationService.class);
    PendingIntent alarmIntent = PendingIntent.getService(context, 0,
        recommendationIntent, 0);

    alarmManager.setInexactRepeating(AlarmManager.ELAPSED_REALTIME_WAKEUP,
        INITIAL_DELAY,
        AlarmManager.INTERVAL_HALF_HOUR,
        alarmIntent);
}
```

After your BroadcastReceiver is complete, you will need to declare both it and RecommendationService in AndroidManifest.xml in the application tag. BootupReceiver will require an intent-filter so that it can listen for the BOOT_COMPLETED intent from the operating system.

```
<service android:name=".RecommendationService"
    android:enabled="true" />

<receiver android:name=".BootupReceiver"
    android:enabled="true"
    android:exported="false">
    <intent-filter>
        <action android:name="android.intent.action.BOOT_COMPLETED"/>
    </intent-filter>
</receiver>
```

You will also need to include the RECEIVE_BOOT_COMPLETE permission declaration at the top of AndroidManifest.xml.

```
<uses-permission android:name="android.permission.RECEIVE_BOOT_COMPLETED" />
```

With MainActivity, RecommendationService, BootupReceiver, and AndroidManifest.xml complete, you should now be able to run your application and see recommendations in the recommendation row. If you are testing your application on an emulator, then your Android TV home screen should look similar to Figure 4-9. If you are testing on a physical device, then your recommendation notifications will be mixed in with the recommendations from other installed applications.

Figure 4-9. Populated recommendations on the Android TV home screen

In this section you have learned about the recommendations row of the Android TV home screen and how to place your own content into it. While you are now able to accomplish this, there are additional features available that you may find helpful in making your application stand out. One of these is the ability to change the background of the Android TV home screen to match your content. This is done by storing a bitmap file with a ContentProvider and accessing it by a URI when your notification is selected. While that is beyond the scope of this book, it does add a nice touch to your app that your users will enjoy. In the next section you will continue to learn about engaging with your users when they are outside of your application by making your data and content searchable through the Android TV global search function.

Android TV Global Search

Another way your users can access your content without going directly to your app is through Android TV's global search functionality. When the users press the microphone button on their controllers or select the search icon in the top left of the Android TV home screen, the system will open a search screen and check to see what installed applications have made data available for searching. In this section you will learn how to use some basic SQLite functionality and how to make your content searchable by using a ContentProvider.

Building the Search Database

In order to make your content available for Android TV global search, you need to create a SQLite table that stores your content information and can be accessed from outside of your application. You will start by writing a handler class for a SQLite database. The purpose of this class is to make accessing the database that you will create easier by using a ContentProvider. Create this class now under your application package directory and name it VideoDatabaseHandler.java. This file will need to declare and initialize multiple properties to the top of the class, as shown here.

```
public class VideoDatabaseHandler {
    private static final String DATABASE_NAME = "video_database_leanback";
    private static final int DATABASE_VERSION = 1;
    private static final String FTS_VIRTUAL_TABLE = "Leanback_table";

    public static final String KEY_NAME =
        SearchManager.SUGGEST_COLUMN_TEXT_1;
    public static final String KEY_DATA_TYPE =
        SearchManager.SUGGEST_COLUMN_CONTENT_TYPE;
```

```
public static final String KEY_PRODUCTION_YEAR =
    SearchManager.SUGGEST_COLUMN_PRODUCTION_YEAR;
public static final String KEY_COLUMN_DURATION =
    SearchManager.SUGGEST_COLUMN_DURATION;
public static final String KEY_ACTION =
    SearchManager.SUGGEST_COLUMN_INTENT_ACTION;
}
```

Here, DATABASE_NAME and DATABASE_VERSION are used for creating your
SQLite database, FTS_VIRTUAL_TABLE contains the name of the table that will
store all of your data, and the rest of the items are keys that will be used to
identify data in the database. Next you will need to make a map of all of the
columns that will be used in your table. You can do this in a new method
named buildColumnMap.

```
private static HashMap<String, String> buildColumnMap() {
    HashMap<String, String> map = new HashMap<String, String>();
    map.put(KEY_NAME, KEY_NAME);
    map.put(KEY_DATA_TYPE, KEY_DATA_TYPE);
    map.put(KEY_PRODUCTION_YEAR, KEY_PRODUCTION_YEAR);
    map.put(KEY_COLUMN_DURATION, KEY_COLUMN_DURATION);
    map.put(KEY_ACTION, KEY_ACTION );
    map.put(BaseColumns._ID, "rowid AS " + BaseColumns._ID);
    map.put(SearchManager.SUGGEST_COLUMN_INTENT_DATA_ID, "rowid AS " +
        SearchManager.SUGGEST_COLUMN_INTENT_DATA_ID);
    map.put(SearchManager.SUGGEST_COLUMN_SHORTCUT_ID, "rowid AS " +
        SearchManager.SUGGEST_COLUMN_SHORTCUT_ID);

    return map;
}
```

Back at the top of VideoDatabaseHandler, you will need to create a new data
item that is initialized using buildColumnMap. This item will be used to create
the projection map for your SQLite query.

```
private static final HashMap<String, String> COLUMN_MAP =
    buildColumnMap();
```

Before you can begin handling queries, you need to create a new inner
class named VideoDatabaseOpenHelper that extends SQLiteOpenHelper
to wrap your database. This inner class will load data into the database
and create the table that will be queried against. When you create
VideoDatabaseOpenHelper, you will also need to include a string that
represents the SQL command for creating your table, a SQLite database,
and a WeakReference containing a Context.

```
private static class VideoDatabaseOpenHelper extends SQLiteOpenHelper {
    private final WeakReference<Context> mHelperContext;
    private SQLiteDatabase mDatabase;

    private static final String FTS_TABLE_CREATE =
            "CREATE VIRTUAL TABLE " + FTS_VIRTUAL_TABLE +
                    " USING fts3 (" +
                    KEY_NAME + ", " +
                    KEY_DATA_TYPE + "," +
                    KEY_ACTION + "," +
                    KEY_PRODUCTION_YEAR + "," +
                    KEY_COLUMN_DURATION + ");";

    public VideoDatabaseOpenHelper(Context context){
        super(context, DATABASE_NAME, null, DATABASE_VERSION);
        mHelperContext = new WeakReference<Context>(context);
    }

    @Override
    public void onCreate(SQLiteDatabase db){
    }

    @Override
    public void onUpgrade(SQLiteDatabase db, int oldVersion, int newVersion){
    }
}
```

> **Note**   You'll notice that the Context for this inner class is stored in a
> WeakReference. Using a static inner class with a WeakReference to the
> Context is a way to avoid memory leaks, as noted in this 2009 Android
> Developers blog post: android-developers.blogspot.com/2009/01/
> avoiding-memory-leaks.html.

Next you will need to complete the onCreate method. This method will store
a reference to the database, create the contents table, and load all of the
searchable items into the database.

```
@Override
public void onCreate(SQLiteDatabase db) {
    mDatabase = db;
    mDatabase.execSQL(FTS_TABLE_CREATE);
    loadDatabase();
}
```

The loadDatabase method will load all of the videos from the data JSON file in your app into your table on a new thread.

```
private void loadDatabase() {
    new Thread(new Runnable() {
        public void run() {
            try {
                loadVideos();
            } catch (IOException e) {
                throw new RuntimeException(e);
            }
        }
    }).start();
}

private void loadVideos() throws IOException {
    List<Video> videos;

    String json = Utils.loadJSONFromResource(mHelperContext.get(),
        R.raw.videos);
    Type collection = new TypeToken<ArrayList<Video>>(){}.getType();

    Gson gson = new Gson();
    videos = gson.fromJson(json, collection);

    for(Video video : videos) {
        addVideoForDeepLink(video);
    }
}

public void addVideoForDeepLink(Video video) {
    ContentValues initialValues = new ContentValues();

    initialValues.put(KEY_NAME, video.getTitle());
    initialValues.put(KEY_DATA_TYPE, "video/mp4");
    initialValues.put(KEY_PRODUCTION_YEAR, "2015");
    initialValues.put(KEY_COLUMN_DURATION, 6400000);

    mDatabase.insert(FTS_VIRTUAL_TABLE, null, initialValues);
}
```

In the addVideoForDeepLink method, you added four values into a ContentValues object. These are the only required items for the information in your table to be searchable. You can add data by adding more columns to your table and including keys from the SearchManager class. Since the sample data for this project does not contain production year or duration of the media, you can use dummy information for this demo application. Once your ContentValues object is populated, you can use it to insert the data for the given video into your table.

At this point your VideoDatabaseOpenHelper inner class is complete. You will need to create a reference to it at the top of VideoDatabaseHandler and initialize it in the class constructor.

```
private final VideoDatabaseOpenHelper mDatabaseOpenHelper;

public VideoDatabaseHandler(Context context) {
    mDatabaseOpenHelper = new VideoDatabaseOpenHelper(context);
}
```

The last thing you need to do in VideoDatabaseHandler is handle queries. There are two more methods that you will add to this class. The first is query, which will take a query passed to it and return a Cursor object containing the search results. The second is getWordMatch, which will accept a string and see if it matches any of the titles in your media data by creating a SQL command to pass to the query method.

```
public Cursor getWordMatch(String query, String[] columns) {
    String selection = KEY_NAME + " MATCH ?";
    String[] selectionArgs = new String[]{query + "*"};

    return query(selection, selectionArgs, columns);
}

private Cursor query(String selection, String[] selectionArgs, String[]
columns) {
    SQLiteQueryBuilder builder = new SQLiteQueryBuilder();
    builder.setTables(FTS_VIRTUAL_TABLE);
    builder.setProjectionMap(COLUMN_MAP);

    Cursor cursor = builder.query(mDatabaseOpenHelper.getReadableDatabase(),
        columns, selection, selectionArgs, null, null, null);

    if (cursor == null) {
        return null;
    } else if (!cursor.moveToFirst()) {
        cursor.close();
        return null;
    }
    return cursor;
}
```

If you have not worked with SQLite before, then this class can seem fairly daunting, but that's okay. While SQLite is out of the scope of this book, I strongly recommend reading through Google's documentation on it. As you become more familiar with databases, it becomes easier to handle data and do some interesting things in the Android platform. If you are already comfortable with SQLite, then you're off to a good start! In the next section, you will create a new ContentProvider to access the database that you have just created and make it available for Android TV global search.

Creating a Global Search Content Provider

Content providers are Android's way of making data from one process available in another. They encapsulate data and provide the tools necessary for securely defining what data can be used by other processes. Create a new Java class and name it VideoContentProvider.java. It will extend the ContentProvider class.

```java
public class VideoContentProvider extends ContentProvider {
    @Override
    public boolean onCreate() {
        return false;
    }

    @Override
    public Cursor query(Uri uri, String[] projection, String selection,
                String[] selectionArgs, String sortOrder) {
        return null;
    }

    @Override
    public String getType(Uri uri) {
        return null;
    }

    @Override
    public Uri insert(Uri uri, ContentValues values) {
        return null;
    }

    @Override
    public int delete(Uri uri, String selection, String[] selectionArgs) {
        return 0;
    }

    @Override
    public int update(Uri uri, ContentValues values, String selection,
    String[] selectionArgs) {
        return 0;
    }
}
```

Next, create a new VideoDatabaseHandler object at the top of the class and initialize it in onCreate.

```
private VideoDatabaseHandler mVideoDatabase;

@Override
public boolean onCreate() {
    mVideoDatabase = new VideoDatabaseHandler(getContext());
    return true;
}
```

The last thing you need to do in VideoContentProvider is flesh out the query method. Luckily, all of the hard work is handled by VideoDatabaseHandler. The only thing you need to do is take the query passed to the content provider from the arguments array, create an array of presenting the data you want back, and then return the Cursor from the getWordMatch method inside of VideoDatabaseHandler.

```
@Override
public Cursor query(Uri uri, String[] projection, String selection, String[] selectionArgs, String sortOrder) {
    String query = selectionArgs[0];

    query = query.toLowerCase();
    String[] columns = new String[]{
            BaseColumns._ID,
            VideoDatabaseHandler.KEY_NAME,
            VideoDatabaseHandler.KEY_DATA_TYPE,
            VideoDatabaseHandler.KEY_PRODUCTION_YEAR,
            VideoDatabaseHandler.KEY_COLUMN_DURATION,
            SearchManager.SUGGEST_COLUMN_INTENT_DATA_ID
    };
    return mVideoDatabase.getWordMatch(query, columns);
}
```

In the next section you learn how to expose your content provider to external processes.

Exposing the Content Provider

With your Java files complete, you will need to set up your application so that other processes can find your content provider. Inside of your res folder, create a new file under the xml directory named searchable.xml. This configuration file will describe your content provider and contain other vital information for Android TV.

```
<searchable xmlns:android="http://schemas.android.com/apk/res/android"
    android:label="@string/app_name"
    android:hint="Search for videos"
    android:searchSettingsDescription="Description"
    android:searchSuggestAuthority="com.apress.mediaplayer"
    android:searchSuggestIntentAction="android.intent.action.VIEW"
    android:searchSuggestIntentData="content://com.apress.mediaplayer/video_
    database_leanback"
    android:searchSuggestSelection=" ?"
    android:searchSuggestThreshold="1"
    android:includeInGlobalSearch="true"
/>
```

When your searchable.xml file is complete, open AndroidManifest.xml
and add the following line in the application node to declare your content
provider in your app.

```
<provider android:name=".VideoContentProvider"
    android:authorities="com.apress.mediaplayer"
    android:exported="true" />
```

Now that your content provider is exposed, you will need to configure your
app so that any items returned from a search will properly open.

Reacting to the Search Action

To finish handling the global search action, you must let the Android TV
system know what to do when one of your items matches a search query.
In AndroidManifest.xml, change the declaration for VideoDetailsActivity
so that it contains an intent-filter for the SEARCH action and points to your
searchable.xml file as metadata.

```
<activity android:name=".VideoDetailsActivity">
    <intent-filter>
        <action android:name="android.intent.action.SEARCH" />
    </intent-filter>

    <meta-data android:name="android.app.searchable"
        android:resource="@xml/searchable" />
</activity>
```

If you run your application now, you will be able to use Android TV's global
search functionality to search for one of your media items by title, as seen in
Figure 4-10.

Figure 4-10. Content found from a global search by title

There is one more problem. If you select that item, your application will crash. This is because VideoDetailsFragment does not know how to handle the situation where no video was passed to it. To remedy this, open VideoDetailsFragment and go into the onCreate method. Immediately after the line that attempts to initialize mVideo from a serialized extra in the intent, add the following block of code:

```
if( mVideo == null ) {
    Intent intent = getActivity().getIntent();
    Uri data = intent.getData();
    String json = Utils.loadJSONFromResource(getActivity(), R.raw.videos);
    Type collection = new TypeToken<ArrayList<Video>>(){}.getType();
    Gson gson = new Gson();
    List<Video> videos = gson.fromJson(json, collection);
    mVideo = videos.get(Integer.parseInt(data.getLastPathSegment())- 1 );
}
```

This will load the data for your app and attempt to find the proper item based on an identifier related to the media item's position in the data. Now if you run your application and use the global search option, you should be able to click on any results from your app and be taken to the proper detail screen for that item.

While there's more you can do to improve this feature, such as add an image for the returned result or include more metadata, you have just completed integrating the demo app with Android TV's global search functionality. You now have a fleshed out Android TV media app, learned how to display content for your users through various components of the Leanback Support library, added a preference screen that can allow users to customize their experience, implemented local and global search, and integrated your features with the Android TV recommendation system.

More Media App Features

While you have learned about many features that can go into an Android TV media application, there's still a lot more that's possible. In this section you will be introduced to some of the additional tools included in the Leanback Support library that can be useful for giving your users a truly enjoyable experience. This section will not go into the full detail for implementing these features, though you should learn enough to be able to find and understand the documentation from Google.

Now Playing Card

If your app plays any sort of media that can continue playing after your users return to the home screen, such as audio, then you must provide a way for the users to return to your app in order to pause or change what's playing. Luckily, Android TV supports this by including a Now Playing card that can appear in the recommendations row of the home screen. You can enable the Now Playing card by creating a MediaSession object from the background service controlling your audio and associating metadata with the session for displaying artwork and information about the playing content. You can also associate a PendingIntent with the Now Playing card so that your application will be launched when the card is selected.

GuidedStepFragment

There will be times when you will want to help your users navigate through a series of decisions. To help with this, Google has provided the GuidedStepFragment in the Leanback Support library that consists of two parts, the guidance view on the right and a list of selectable items on the left. The guidance view will let you prompt your users so that they can figure out what they want to select from the list of options. An example of the GuidedStepFragment is the systems settings on the Android TV home screen, which can allow users to dive through multiple levels of options per category.

Live Channels

Since users are familiar with the experience of browsing through channels to find something to watch, you can present your own data in this fashion by using the TV Input Framework. This will allow you to create channels for streaming your content to your users alongside content from hardware sources and other apps by utilizing another ContentProvider and services. Users will be able to browse all channels by using the Android TV Live Channels application installed on their devices.

Summary

In this chapter you learned about additional features that you can implement in your own media applications to enrich experiences and provide a valuable tool for your users. You added searching both locally in the app and through the global search functionality of Android TV. You also learned about the Leanback styled preference fragment for your app, and how to engage with users when they are not in your app through the Android TV recommendations system. Outside of the topics you made work with your own demo, you were introduced to three features that provide you with more possibilities for creating an amazing user experience. In the next chapter you will learn about a few tools that will help you create better gaming experiences for the Android-powered television.

Chapter 5

The Android TV Platform for Game Development

While media apps make up a significant portion of the Android TV app ecosystem, games account for roughly 90% of the revenue developers receive from the Play Store. Understanding how to get your games working and ready for Android TV is vital if you are a game developer or hobbyist who would like to have an extra avenue for making a profit off of your work. Thankfully, since Android TV is a fully functioning Android OS, it doesn't take much to migrate your games over to the new platform. This chapter will focus on Android TV and some tools for building your games with the platform, as developing complete games is an extensive topic and outside the scope of this book. This chapter will also only discuss Android development, though other popular game engines are known to work with the Android TV.

Android TV Games vs. Mobile

Although developing games for Android TV is very similar to developing for mobile phones and tablets, there are a couple of things that you will need to be aware of so that your games work as expected and are enjoyable by your users. First and foremost, your app should work in landscape mode. While phones and tablets tend to be used in portrait mode with the possibility of being used in landscape, televisions are almost always going to be in landscape orientation. As such, you need to make sure your games will work as expected and use screen space wisely. The second thing that you should consider is that the television is a central screen that is shared among players in a room. If you have a card or strategy game, it's imperative that your players be able to hide their actions from each other. One of the best ways to solve this problem is by creating a second screen experience through the use of phones and tablets, allowing players to perform their actions in private, and then updating the game screen on the television.

Manifest Setup

As discussed in Chapter 2, there are separate rows for displaying media applications and games on the Android TV. In order to have your game displayed in the games row, you must declare your app as a game in the application node of AndroidManifest.xml.

```
<application
    android:allowBackup="true"
    android:icon="@mipmap/ic_launcher"
    android:label="@string/app_name"
    android:isGame="true"
    android:theme="@style/AppTheme">
```

If your game will support the use of the Android TV gamepad controller, then you will also need to declare that feature inside of your application. You can do this by adding a new uses-feature node at the top of your manifest.

```
<uses-feature android:name="android.hardware.gamepad"
    android:required="false" />
```

You'll notice that the required field in this node is set to false. If this field is set to true, then your app will not be installable on Android TV devices. Other than these very small changes, the rest of your manifest will work exactly like it would for a standard mobile application.

Gamepad Controller Input

While your media application used simplified navigation to support a D-pad, your games can support the gamepad controller to allow for far more elaborate interactions. There are two main types of input that can come from a gamepad controller: digital and analog. Digital inputs include buttons, which have either a pressed or unpressed state. The analog inputs consist of the joysticks or triggers on the controller and can provide values within a set range. In this section you will learn how to read input from a gamepad controller so that you can provide your users with a better gaming experience on Android TV.

Setting Up the Controller Demo Project

You will learn about the gamepad controller through the use of a new sample application that accepts input from the game controller and displays the state the controls on the screen. The source code for this application can be found on the Apress web page for this book (www. apress.com/9781484217832). You can also create this project yourself by creating a new empty Android TV application in Android Studio and setting up AndroidManifest.xml, as discussed in the last section. The layout file, activity_main.xml in this case, will consists of multiple TextView objects that will either provide a label or be changed to show the value of their associated input. While the following sample code only represents one item, the rest should be fairly straightforward to figure out when you see the Java code, and so are excluded here to conserve space.

```
...
<RelativeLayout
    android:layout_width="match_parent"
    android:layout_height="wrap_content">

    <TextView
        android:id="@+id/label_a"
        android:layout_width="wrap_content"
        android:layout_height="wrap_content"
        android:text="Button A: "/>

    <TextView
        android:id="@+id/button_a"
        android:layout_toRightOf="@+id/label_a"
        android:layout_width="wrap_content"
        android:layout_height="wrap_content"
        android:text="@string/state_not_pressed"/>

</RelativeLayout>
...
```

This sample will also use two additional values in strings.xml to represent the pressed and unpressed states for buttons:

```
<string name="state_pressed">is pressed.</string>
<string name="state_not_pressed">is not pressed.</string>
```

Next you will need to modify MainActivity.java so that it contains references to all of the views that will be changeable from your layout file and associates them with the correct views.

```java
private TextView mButtonStateA;
private TextView mButtonStateB;
private TextView mButtonStateX;
private TextView mButtonStateY;
private TextView mButtonStateR1;
private TextView mButtonStateL1;

private TextView mJoystickState1AxisX;
private TextView mJoystickState1AxisY;
private TextView mJoystickState2AxisX;
private TextView mJoystickState2AxisY;

@Override
protected void onCreate(Bundle savedInstanceState) {
    super.onCreate(savedInstanceState);
    setContentView(R.layout.activity_main);

    mButtonStateA = (TextView) findViewById(R.id.button_a);
    mButtonStateB = (TextView) findViewById(R.id.button_b);
    mButtonStateX = (TextView) findViewById(R.id.button_x);
    mButtonStateY = (TextView) findViewById(R.id.button_y);
    mButtonStateR1 = (TextView) findViewById(R.id.button_r1);
    mButtonStateL1 = (TextView) findViewById(R.id.button_l1);

    mJoystickState1AxisX = (TextView)findViewById(R.id.joystick_1_axis_x);
    mJoystickState1AxisY = (TextView)findViewById(R.id.joystick_1_axis_y);
    mJoystickState2AxisX = (TextView)findViewById(R.id.joystick_2_axis_x);
    mJoystickState2AxisY = (TextView)findViewById(R.id.joystick_2_axis_y);
}
```

Once you have completed your layout and stored a reference to the key views, you should be able to run your application and see a screen similar to Figure 5-1. It should be noted that while you can run this program on the emulator, you will need an actual gamepad controller and an Android TV device to test the code in rest of this section.

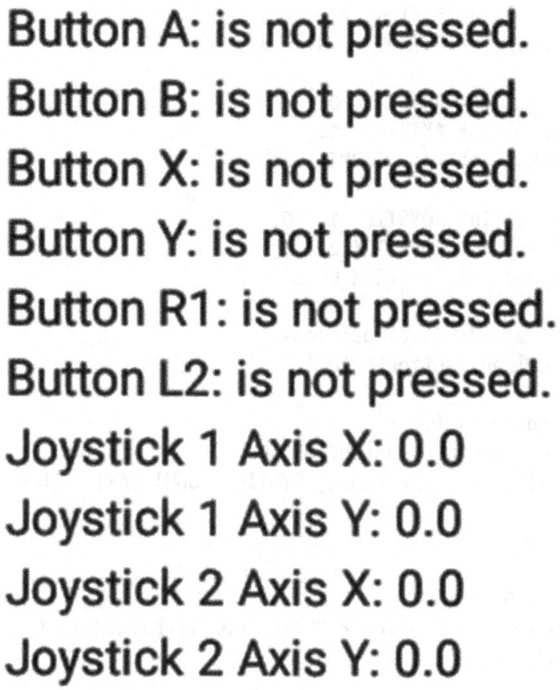

Button A: is not pressed.
Button B: is not pressed.
Button X: is not pressed.
Button Y: is not pressed.
Button R1: is not pressed.
Button L2: is not pressed.
Joystick 1 Axis X: 0.0
Joystick 1 Axis Y: 0.0
Joystick 2 Axis X: 0.0
Joystick 2 Axis Y: 0.0

Figure 5-1. Gamepad controller demo layout

Storing Controller Inputs

To simplify the process of maintaining the controller state, you will create a new utility class for this sample project called GameController.java. This class will store data whenever an analog or digital control input event is received and will provide helper methods for your application to determine what controls are currently being used.

Once you have GameController.java created, you will need to make new data items representing the buttons and joysticks on the controller, as well as values that will help those data items map to the controller correctly. When the GameController object is instantiated, you will initialize the button and joystick state objects, then provide them with default values.

```
public static final int BUTTON_A = 0;
public static final int BUTTON_B = 1;
public static final int BUTTON_X = 2;
public static final int BUTTON_Y = 3;
public static final int BUTTON_R1 = 4;
public static final int BUTTON_R2 = 5;
public static final int BUTTON_L1 = 6;
```

```
public static final int BUTTON_L2 = 7;
public static final int BUTTON_COUNT = 8;

public static final int AXIS_X = 0;
public static final int AXIS_Y = 1;
public static final int AXIS_COUNT = 2;

public static final int JOYSTICK_1 = 0;
public static final int JOYSTICK_2 = 1;
public static final int JOYSTICK_COUNT = 2;

private final float mJoystickPositions[][];
private final boolean mButtonState[];

public GameController() {
    mButtonState = new boolean[BUTTON_COUNT];
    mJoystickPositions = new float[JOYSTICK_COUNT][AXIS_COUNT];
    resetState();
}

private void resetState() {
    for (int button = 0; button < BUTTON_COUNT; button++) {
        mButtonState[button] = false;
    }

    for (int joystick = 0; joystick < JOYSTICK_COUNT; joystick++) {
        for (int axis = 0; axis < AXIS_COUNT; axis++) {
            mJoystickPositions[joystick][axis] = 0.0f;
        }
    }
}
```

With your data items created and initialized, you will need a way to change their values. When a KeyEvent (for button presses) or MotionEvent (for analog inputs) is received by the application, it will be forwarded to this utility class. You can then determine what control was used in order to save its state. For a button, you will determine if the button is currently being held down, then you will save that information in the array of button states.

```
public void handleKeyEvent(KeyEvent keyEvent) {
    boolean keyIsDown = keyEvent.getAction() == KeyEvent.ACTION_DOWN;

    if (keyEvent.getKeyCode() == KeyEvent.KEYCODE_BUTTON_A) {
        mButtonState[BUTTON_A] = keyIsDown;
    } else if (keyEvent.getKeyCode() == KeyEvent.KEYCODE_BUTTON_B) {
        mButtonState[BUTTON_B] = keyIsDown;
```

```
    } else if (keyEvent.getKeyCode() == KeyEvent.KEYCODE_BUTTON_X) {
        mButtonState[BUTTON_X] = keyIsDown;
    } else if (keyEvent.getKeyCode() == KeyEvent.KEYCODE_BUTTON_Y) {
        mButtonState[BUTTON_Y] = keyIsDown;
    } else if (keyEvent.getKeyCode() == KeyEvent.KEYCODE_BUTTON_R1 ) {
        mButtonState[BUTTON_R1] = keyIsDown;
    } else if (keyEvent.getKeyCode() == KeyEvent.KEYCODE_BUTTON_R2 ) {
        mButtonState[BUTTON_R2] = keyIsDown;
    } else if (keyEvent.getKeyCode() == KeyEvent.KEYCODE_BUTTON_L1 ) {
        mButtonState[BUTTON_L1] = keyIsDown;
    } else if (keyEvent.getKeyCode() == KeyEvent.KEYCODE_BUTTON_L2 ) {
        mButtonState[BUTTON_L2] = keyIsDown;
    }
}
```

Similarly, when a joystick is moved, you will save its X and Y axes positions.

```
public void handleMotionEvent(MotionEvent motionEvent) {
    mJoystickPositions[JOYSTICK_1][AXIS_X] =
        motionEvent.getAxisValue( MotionEvent.AXIS_X );
    mJoystickPositions[JOYSTICK_1][AXIS_Y] =
        motionEvent.getAxisValue( MotionEvent.AXIS_Y );

    mJoystickPositions[JOYSTICK_2][AXIS_X] =
        motionEvent.getAxisValue( MotionEvent.AXIS_Z );
    mJoystickPositions[JOYSTICK_2][AXIS_Y] =
        motionEvent.getAxisValue( MotionEvent.AXIS_RZ );
}
```

Now that your utility class can store state information for the gamepad controller, you will need to provide a way to access that information across your application. You can do this by creating two getter methods that return the state for any button or joystick that you keep track of on the controller.

```
public float getJoystickPosition(int joystickIndex, int axis) {
    return mJoystickPositions[joystickIndex][axis];
}

public boolean isButtonDown(int buttonId) {
    return mButtonState[buttonId];
}
```

When your GameController utility class is complete, you will need to be able to feed data to it from the physical gamepad controller. How you retrieve this input will vary depending on your application. If you use a view to listen for the controller events, then you will need to override the following methods:

```
onGenericMotionEvent( MotionEvent event )
onKeyDown( int keyCode, KeyEvent event )
onKeyUp( int keyCode, KeyEvent event )
```

If you use an activity for receiving the input events, then you will only need to override two methods:

```
dispatchGenericMotionEvent( MotionEvent event )
dispatchKeyEvent( KeyEvent event )
```

For this sample, you will use MainActivity to retrieve events from the gamepad controller, so will only need to override the two methods mentioned above. Before you start receiving input from the controller, you will need to create a new instance of the GameController utility object at the top of your class.

```
private final GameController mController = new GameController();
```

To retrieve analog inputs from the joysticks or triggers on a controller, you will use dispatchGenericMotionEvent. In this method, you will pass the MotionEvent to mController, then you will update the views representing the values of your joysticks by checking the joystick positions.

```
@Override
public boolean dispatchGenericMotionEvent(MotionEvent ev) {
    mController.handleMotionEvent(ev);

    //R2 and L2 (triggers) are also analog and use this callback
    mJoystickState1AxisX.setText(String.valueOf(
            mController.getJoystickPosition(GameController.JOYSTICK_1,
                    GameController.AXIS_X)));
    mJoystickState1AxisY.setText(String.valueOf(
            mController.getJoystickPosition(GameController.JOYSTICK_1,
                    GameController.AXIS_Y)));
    mJoystickState2AxisX.setText(String.valueOf(
            mController.getJoystickPosition(GameController.JOYSTICK_2,
                    GameController.AXIS_X)));
    mJoystickState2AxisY.setText(String.valueOf(
            mController.getJoystickPosition(GameController.JOYSTICK_2,
                    GameController.AXIS_Y)));
    return true;
}
```

dispatchKeyEvent is called whenever a key is pressed or released. In this method you will pass the KeyEvent to mController and then update the appropriate TextView to reflect the event. You will notice this example has a special case for the back key. When that button is pressed, the users have an expectation for how it should act, so you should allow the system to handle it rather than creating your own response.

```
@Override
public boolean dispatchKeyEvent(KeyEvent event) {
    if( event.getKeyCode() == KeyEvent.KEYCODE_BACK ) {
        return super.dispatchKeyEvent(event);
    }

    mController.handleKeyEvent(event);

    updateTextViewForButton( mButtonStateA,
        mController.isButtonDown( GameController.BUTTON_A ) );
    updateTextViewForButton( mButtonStateB,
        mController.isButtonDown( GameController.BUTTON_B ) );
    updateTextViewForButton( mButtonStateX,
        mController.isButtonDown( GameController.BUTTON_X ) );
    updateTextViewForButton( mButtonStateY,
        mController.isButtonDown( GameController.BUTTON_Y ) );
    updateTextViewForButton( mButtonStateR1,
        mController.isButtonDown( GameController.BUTTON_R1 ) );
    updateTextViewForButton( mButtonStateL1,
        mController.isButtonDown( GameController.BUTTON_L1 ) );

    return true;
}

private void updateTextViewForButton( TextView textView, boolean pressed ) {
    if( pressed ) {
        textView.setText( getString( R.string.state_pressed ) );
    } else {
        textView.setText( getString( R.string.state_not_pressed ) );
    }
}
```

Now you should be able to run this sample application on a physical Android TV device and see how your app responds to input from a gamepad controller, as shown in Figure 5-2.

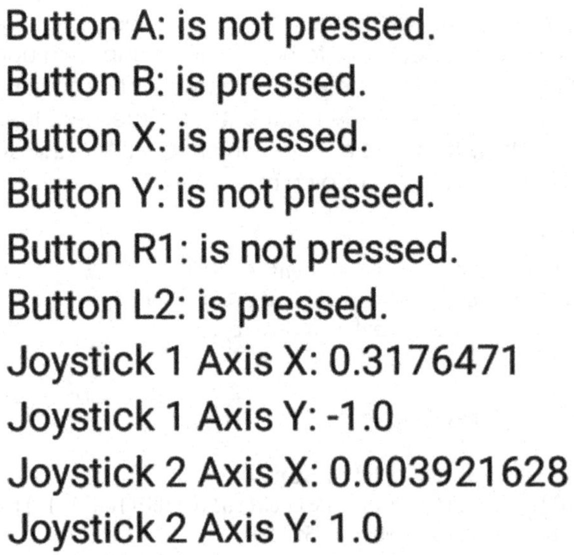

Button A: is not pressed.

Button B: is pressed.

Button X: is pressed.

Button Y: is not pressed.

Button R1: is not pressed.

Button L2: is pressed.

Joystick 1 Axis X: 0.3176471

Joystick 1 Axis Y: -1.0

Joystick 2 Axis X: 0.003921628

Joystick 2 Axis Y: 1.0

Figure 5-2. Gamepad control input demonstration

Controller Best Practices

In the sample app for this section you have learned how to work with some of the features for the Android TV gamepad controller. While understanding how to use the controller is important, you should also follow these best practices to ensure that your users have an excellent experience when using your application. Google has provided a few key points to help you make the most out of your app:

- Let your users know as soon as possible if a controller is necessary. This is best done in the Google Play Store description. If users are not aware that they need a controller and run into difficulty using your app because of it, they may give your app a poor rating.

- Users expect certain buttons to perform certain actions, such as the A button triggering an Accept action, and the B button canceling an action. The closer you stick to these expectations, the happier your users will be.

- Verify controller hardware requirements. If your app uses a controller gyroscope or triggers to perform actions, but the users have a controller that is lacking the required hardware, then your app will not work as expected. Be sure to have a backup plan to support these users.

■ As obvious as this may seem, you will need to make sure that your app handles multiple controllers for multiplayer games. While the sample app for this section did not cover this, you should be able to detect the device ID for each input event received by your app and respond accordingly.

■ When a game controller disconnects in the middle of gameplay for any reason, including Bluetooth dropping or the controller running out of power, you should respond by pausing the game and informing the users that they have been disconnected. You could also provide a dialog to help them troubleshoot the problem.

■ If possible, display visual instructions for using the controller. Google provides an Android TV gamepad template on its documentation page that can be used for this purpose.

Note   A download link for the Android TV gamepad template is available under "Show Controller Instructions" in the "Building TV Games" article at http://developer.android.com/training/tv/games/index.html.

Using the Local Area Network

As mentioned earlier in this chapter, some games require a certain level of secrecy between players. One of the best ways to facilitate this is by using mobile phones or tablets as a second screen, allowing each player to secretly plan his or her actions. To help create this experience, Google has created the Nearby Connections API, which allows devices on the same local area network (LAN) to easily communicate. In the context of an Android TV game, the television would act as a central host, and each second screen device would act as a client.

Setting Up a Second Screen Project

For the second screen experience to work, you will need two applications: one for the television and one for mobile devices. When you create the project for this sample, you will create a module for both device types, as shown in Figure 5-3.

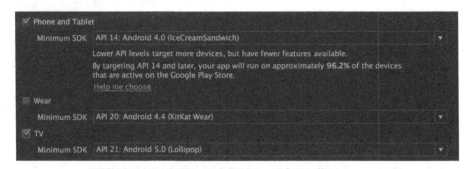

Figure 5-3. Android Studio module creation screen

The mobile module can use the Empty Activity option with the default settings, and when you build the TV module you can select the Add No Activity option. Once both modules are created, you will need to create a new MainActivity.java file for the TV module and add it to the module's AndroidManifest.xml, similar to what you did in Chapter 3.

When your initial projects are created and you can install the mobile module on a mobile device and the TV module on an Android TV, you can move on to the next step. Because the Nearby Connections API is a part of Play Services, you will need to include the Play Services library in the build. gradle file for each module under the dependencies node.

```
compile 'com.google.android.gms:play-services:8.3.0'
```

Within the AndroidManifest.xml files for both modules, you need to request the ACCESS_NETWORK_STATE and WAKE_LOCK permissions.

```
<uses-permission android:name="android.permission.ACCESS_NETWORK_STATE" />
<uses-permission android:name="android.permission.WAKE_LOCK" />
```

Next you need to declare a piece of metadata in the application node that will define the service ID that the Nearby Connections API will use for connecting devices over the LAN.

```
<meta-data android:name="com.google.android.gms.nearby.connection.
SERVICE_ID"
    android:value="@string/service_id" />
```

Here, service_id is a string for both modules so that each app can identify the other on the network. You can add that string to strings.xml now.

```
<string name="service_id">Apress Service Id</string>
```

Once you are done in the AndroidManifest.xml and strings.xml files, you can close both for each module. Inside of MainActivity. java for both modules you will need to create a new GoogleApiClient and connect to it. Start by implementing the ConnectionCallbacks and OnConnectionFailedListener interfaces in your activity.

```
public class MainActivity extends Activity implements
        GoogleApiClient.ConnectionCallbacks,
        GoogleApiClient.OnConnectionFailedListener {

    @Override
    public void onConnected(Bundle bundle) {
    }

    @Override
    public void onConnectionSuspended(int i) {
    }

    @Override
    public void onConnectionFailed(ConnectionResult connectionResult) {
    }
}
```

Next, define your GoogleApiClient at the top of the class and initialize it in onCreate. Once your GoogleApiClient is set up, you can connect to it in onStart. You will also want to disconnect from the GoogleApiClient in onStop.

```
private GoogleApiClient mGoogleApiClient;
@Override
protected void onCreate(Bundle savedInstanceState) {
    super.onCreate(savedInstanceState);
    mGoogleApiClient = new GoogleApiClient.Builder( this )
            .addConnectionCallbacks( this )
            .addOnConnectionFailedListener( this )
            .addApi( Nearby.CONNECTIONS_API )
            .build();
}
@Override
protected void onStart() {
    super.onStart();
    mGoogleApiClient.connect();
}

@Override
protected void onStop() {
    super.onStop();
```

```
if( mGoogleApiClient != null && mGoogleApiClient.isConnected() ) {
    disconnect();
    mGoogleApiClient.disconnect();
}
}
```

Inside of onStop you'll notice that there's an additional call to a method named disconnect. For now, create a stub for that method in both MainActivity files.

The last piece of code that is used by both apps is a helper method for determining if the application is connected to a LAN through wireless or an Ethernet cable. First you need to define an array of integers representing the two network types.

```
private static int[] NETWORK_TYPES = {
        ConnectivityManager.TYPE_WIFI,
        ConnectivityManager.TYPE_ETHERNET
};
```

After you have created NETWORK_TYPES, you can add a new method called isConnectedToNetwork that checks to see if the device is connected to either network type.

```
private boolean isConnectedToNetwork() {
    ConnectivityManager connectivityManager = (ConnectivityManager)
        getSystemService( Context.CONNECTIVITY_SERVICE );
    for( int networkType : NETWORK_TYPES ) {
        NetworkInfo info = connectivityManager.getNetworkInfo(networkType);
        if( info != null && info.isConnectedOrConnecting() ) {
            return true;
        }
    }
    return false;
}
```

At this point your TV and mobile module should look almost identical. In the next section you learn how to modify the TV module so that it advertises over the LAN and properly responds to connection requests.

Advertising over the LAN

When you create a second screen experience for your users, you will use the television app as a host for incoming connections. In order for those incoming connections (known as clients or peers) to find the host, it will need to advertise its availability over the network. The host will also need to be able to respond to connection requests and send messages over the LAN. In the TV module's `MainActivity.java`, implement `ConnectionRequestListener` and `MessageListener` with stubs for their required methods.

```
public class MainActivity extends Activity implements
    GoogleApiClient.ConnectionCallbacks,
    GoogleApiClient.OnConnectionFailedListener,
    Connections.ConnectionRequestListener,
    Connections.MessageListener
```

Next you will need to add two new values to the top of the class: a constant long value that will be used for defining the length of time the app should advertise, and a list of string objects that will store the ID for each peer connected to the host.

```
private static final long CONNECTION_TIME_OUT = 60000L;
private List<String> mRemotePeerEndpoints = new ArrayList<String>();
```

Next you will need to start advertising on the network. For this sample you will start advertising as soon as the `GoogleApiClient` has finished connecting, though in a real app you would not start advertising until you were ready to connect clients to the host.

```
@Override
public void onConnected(Bundle bundle) {
    advertise();
}
```

The `advertise` method will ensure that the device is connected to a network, and then start advertising using the Nearby Connections API. This API provides a callback that will let you check the result of the advertisement so that your app can react appropriately if it is successful or not.

```
private void advertise() {
    if( !isConnectedToNetwork() )
        return;

    String name = "Nearby Advertising";

    Nearby.Connections.startAdvertising(mGoogleApiClient, name, null,
    CONNECTION_TIME_OUT, this).setResultCallback(
        new ResultCallback<Connections.StartAdvertisingResult>() {
        @Override
```

```
        public void onResult(Connections.StartAdvertisingResult result) {
            if (result.getStatus().isSuccess()) {
                Log.v( "Apress", "Successfully advertising" );
            }
        }
    });
}
```

Now that your TV application is able to advertise, it will need to respond to connection requests from mobile devices. In the onConnectionRequest method, you can determine if you want to connect to a device based on the information passed as arguments. For this sample you will simply connect to anything that has responded to your service ID advertisements. When you have connected, you will save the remote device ID in a list so that you can communicate with that device through the life of the connection.

```
@Override
public void onConnectionRequest(final String remoteEndpointId,
    final String remoteDeviceId,
    final String remoteEndpointName,
    byte[] payload) {
    Nearby.Connections.acceptConnectionRequest( mGoogleApiClient,
        remoteEndpointId, payload, this ).setResultCallback(
            new ResultCallback<Status>() {
        @Override
        public void onResult(Status status) {
            if( status.isSuccess() ) {
                getWindow().addFlags(
                    WindowManager.LayoutParams.FLAG_KEEP_SCREEN_ON);
                if( !mRemotePeerEndpoints.contains( remoteEndpointId ) ) {
                    mRemotePeerEndpoints.add( remoteEndpointId );
                }
            } else {
                Log.e( "Apress", "onConnectionRequest failed: " +
                    status.getStatusMessage() );
            }
        }
    });
}
```

You'll notice that when a client has been successfully connected, the device requests to keep the screen awake. This is because receiving messages from a client will not count as an input event, so this method will prevent the TV from going to sleep while your users are playing your game. When you have connected clients to the host, you will be able to receive and send messages back and forth between the devices. The onMessageReceived method will be called whenever the client sends a message payload to the host. For this sample you will simply place the payload into a Toast message, and then echo it out to all client.

```
@Override
public void onMessageReceived(String s, byte[] bytes, boolean b) {
    Toast.makeText(this, new String(bytes), Toast.LENGTH_SHORT).show();
    Nearby.Connections.sendReliableMessage( mGoogleApiClient,
        mRemotePeerEndpoints, bytes );
}
```

The final thing you need to do with the host application is properly disconnect when the activity calls onStop. To do this you will need to expand on the disconnect stub method that you created earlier so that it stops the application from advertising and severs all peer connections.

```
private void disconnect() {
    Nearby.Connections.stopAdvertising(mGoogleApiClient);
    Nearby.Connections.stopAllEndpoints(mGoogleApiClient);
    mRemotePeerEndpoints.clear();
}
```

If you were to run your application now, you would only see a blank screen, as this app only advertises on its own, but requires clients in order to respond to their connection requests or messages.

Discovering Over the LAN

While having a host application set up is great, you still need to create a client app to be able to communicate between a second screen and the television. You can get started by opening the MainActivity.java file within the mobile module and adding the two additional interfaces that will be necessary for a client—MessageListener and EndpointDiscoveryListener. Once you have created the required methods for those two interfaces, you will need a few new member objects. The first is a string that will store the ID for a host endpoint that you have connected to. The other objects are a handler and runnable that will periodically send messages over the Nearby Connections API to the host device.

```
private String mRemoteHostEndpoint;
private Handler mHandler = new Handler();
private Runnable mRunnable = new Runnable() {
    @Override
    public void run() {
        if ( !TextUtils.isEmpty( mRemoteHostEndpoint ) ) {
            Nearby.Connections.sendReliableMessage(mGoogleApiClient,
```

```
                        mRemoteHostEndpoint, "Hello World".getBytes() );
            mHandler.postDelayed(this, 5000);
        }
    }
};
```

While this code snippet uses the sendReliableMessage method, you can also send messages that aren't guaranteed to be delivered. As with anything in software development, there is always a trade-off. Sending unreliable messages will have a lower overhead, whereas reliable messages will always be delivered if the recipient can be found.

Next you can add a call to a new method named discoverHost as soon as the app's Google API client has finished connecting.

```
@Override
public void onConnected(Bundle bundle) {
    discoverHost();
}
```

The first thing discoverHost will do is ensure that the mobile device is connected to the local network. After the network connection has been verified, this method will use the Nearby Connections API to attempt to discover advertising hosts on the LAN. The third argument passed into the startDiscovery method will tell the API to only attempt discovery for 60 seconds. Once the app has either started discovery or failed, you will receive a Status object in the resultant callback.

```
private void discoverHost() {
    if( !isConnectedToNetwork() ) {
        return;
    }

    String serviceId = getString( R.string.service_id );
    Nearby.Connections.startDiscovery(mGoogleApiClient, serviceId,
        60000L, this)
            .setResultCallback( new ResultCallback<Status>() {
        @Override
        public void onResult(Status status) {
            if (status.isSuccess()) {
                Log.v("Apress", "Started discovering");
            }
        }
    });
}
```

When a host is discovered, the onEndpointFound method will be called by the Nearby Connections API. In this method you will send a connection request to the host with a new callback. If the host accepts your connection request, you will be notified so that you can stop discovery. At this point you can start sending messages to the host when appropriate for your application. For simplicity, this sample application will use the Handler and Runnable that you defined earlier in this section to send the text "Hello World" to the host every five seconds.

```
@Override
public void onEndpointFound(String endpointId, String deviceId,
    final String serviceId, String endpointName) {

    byte[] payload = null;

    Nearby.Connections.sendConnectionRequest( mGoogleApiClient, deviceId,
        endpointId, payload,
            new Connections.ConnectionResponseCallback() {
        @Override
        public void onConnectionResponse(String s, Status status,
            byte[] bytes) {
            if( status.isSuccess() ) {
                getWindow().addFlags(
                    WindowManager.LayoutParams.FLAG_KEEP_SCREEN_ON);
                Nearby.Connections.stopDiscovery(mGoogleApiClient,
                    serviceId);
                mRemoteHostEndpoint = s;
                mHandler.post( mRunnable );
            } else {
                Log.e( "Apress", "Connection to endpoint failed" );
            }
        }
    }, this );

}
```

As with the host application, you have implemented MessageListener in the client app. When a message is received from another device, onMessageReceived will be called. In this sample application you will take the byte array payload and convert it into a string, then display it as a Toast message.

```
@Override
public void onMessageReceived(String s, byte[] bytes, boolean b) {
    Toast.makeText( this, new String( bytes ), Toast.LENGTH_SHORT ).show();
}
```

The last thing you need to do in your client app is handle disconnecting from the host. Inside of your onStop method, you should have a call to disconnect. This method will verify that your device is connected to the LAN, and then either stop attempting to discover host devices or disconnect from any host device that is connected.

```
private void disconnect() {
    if( !isConnectedToNetwork() )
        return;

    if( TextUtils.isEmpty(mRemoteHostEndpoint) ) {
        Nearby.Connections.stopDiscovery( mGoogleApiClient,
            getString( R.string.service_id ) );
    } else {
        Nearby.Connections.disconnectFromEndpoint( mGoogleApiClient,
            mRemoteHostEndpoint );
        mRemoteHostEndpoint = null;
    }
}
```

Now that you have a host and client application created, you should install the TV module onto your Android TV device and your mobile module onto a tablet or phone. If both devices are connected to the same LAN, they should automatically find and connect to each other. Once the connection has been established, data will begin periodically sending between the two devices and being displayed in a Toast message, as seen in Figure 5-4.

Figure 5-4. *Toast message on the Android TV from a received message payload*

In this section you have learned about the Nearby Connections API and how to create a host and client application. This will let you easily set up second screen experiences for your application so that users can use mobile devices to plan their actions and send that information to the television. In the next section you will be introduced to a few new APIs available in Google Play Game Services.

Google Play Game Services

As you more than likely know, Google has provided an excellent suite of APIs and tools for Android development in the Google Play Services library. With that exists Google Play Game Services, which is a set of classes focused on helping game developers easily create apps that their users will enjoy. While going in depth into Google Play Game Services and how to use it is far beyond the scope of this book, and worthy of a book in and of itself, you should at least be aware of some of the capabilities it offers so that you can enhance your Android TV games.

Achievements

Achievements are a core part of Android games and are an easy way to reward players for enjoying your game. They can also be used to spur friendly competition between players as they attempt to get more achievements than their friends. You have a few different options when adding achievements to your game, as they can either be instantly awarded for performing an action, or iteratively so that players must complete a specific task multiple times. Achievements may also be hidden so that the users do not know they exist before being earned. At least five achievements are required in a game before it can be published.

Leaderboards

Leaderboards provide a great way to show players how well they are performing in your game compared to other players. For your hardcore player base it provides them with an opportunity to fight for the top position, whereas your more casual players can compare how they're doing with their friends. If you have variations within your game (such as different maps in a strategy game), you can use multiple leaderboards so that players can see how they compare across each variant.

Saved Games

One of the biggest hassles for gamers who own multiple devices is being locked to a specific device in order to finish their game. If you have a game that can work on the television as well as a handheld device, you should implement the Saved Games API. This will allow you to take a snapshot of data and save it online so that players can maintain their progress as they switch between various platforms or upgrade to new devices.

Multiplayer

While you have learned about the Nearby Connections API earlier in this chapter, it only supports local multiplayer games. Using Google Play Game Services, you can support online multiplayers for real-time and turn-based games. Google automatically manages connections, provides a player selection user interface, and stores state information for players and rooms during the game session.

Quests and Events

Events can be triggered by in-game player actions and sent to Google's game servers for you to analyze. This can be useful for determining which areas of your game may be too easy or too difficult so that you can adjust them for your users. The quests service uses the events feature so that you can engage players through time-bound challenges. When players complete these challenges, you can reward them. One of the largest advantages of the quest system is that as long as you are collecting events from the game, you can publish new quests for your users without having to push an updated version of your app to the Play Store.

Summary

In this chapter you learned about some of the tools that you can use to create or port your games to the Android TV platform. You learned about the controller and how to read input from it, how to provide a second screen experience through local networking, and some of the features of Google Play Game Services that can enrich the game experience for your players. While game development is beyond the scope of this book, you should have a strong understanding of how to make your games work with Android TV.

Chapter 6

Android TV App Publishing

After you have built an application, you always want to do a final run-through to ensure that your app works as expected. With Android TV this is especially important, as each Android TV app is subject to approval before being available on the Google Play Store. In this chapter you will learn about the items that Google will look for when evaluating your app and some general tips for distributing your app to users.

Android TV App Checklist

It is important to note that the approval process isn't for censorship, but rather to make sure your app layouts and controls work correctly for Android TV users. Before you attempt to upload your APK to the Play Store, you should validate that your app meets Google's guidelines.

Support the Android TV OS

In order for users to access your application from the Android TV home screen, you will need to make sure that you provide an Android TV entry point into your app by declaring a CATEGORY_LEANBACK_LAUNCHER filter in an activity node of your manifest. If this is not available, then your application will not appear in either of the application rows on the home screen.

When you have declared an activity for Android TV, you will need to associate a banner icon with it that will be displayed in the application row. The launcher banner will need to be 320px by 180px and any text on the image will need to be localized for every language that your application supports.

If you are porting an application from strictly mobile to Android TV, then you will need to ensure that your manifest does not declare any required hardware that is not supported by the Android TV platform. This includes the camera, touchscreen, and various hardware sensors. If any of these items are declared as required, your app will not be discoverable by Android TV devices.

UI Design

In an episode of the Android Backstage podcast, former Android TV team engineer Tim Kilbourn mentioned an app that had been released for the Google TV platform without verifying that it worked as expected. Rather than displaying in a presentable fashion, the app was locked into portrait mode and stretched across the television. Experiences like this are why UI verification are an important part of the Android TV approval process. Needless to say, you should ensure that your app provides layout resources that work in landscape orientation.

Because most users will experience their television from an average of ten feet away, you will need to ensure that all text and controls are large enough to be visible, and all bitmaps and icons are high resolution. Due to some unique conditions of TV, you will also need to make sure your layouts handle overscan and your application's color scheme works well. These topics were discussed in Chapter 2 in greater detail.

If your application uses advertisements, it is recommended that you use video ads that are full-screen and dismissible within 30 seconds. It is important to note that advertisements that rely on sending an intent to a web page should not be used, as Android TV does not come with a built-in web browser. If you do launch an intent for a web page, your application will crash if the users have not installed their own web browsers.

You must also make sure your app responds correctly to the D-pad or game controller so that your users can navigate through your application. This is handled by the classes in the Leanback Support library, but you will need to make sure your own custom classes also respond accordingly.

Searching and Discovery

While having an application that plays content is one thing, you can take it to an entirely new level by helping users discover content or by providing recommendations. These items were covered in depth in Chapter 4. In short, you should make sure global search and recommendations are working for your applications, and users should be taken directly to the content when they find something that they are interested in.

Games

In the last chapter you were introduced to some key points for Android TV game development. When you create a game for Android TV, you will need to declare it as a game in the manifest for it to show up in the games row on the home screen.

Your manifest should also be updated if you support the use of the game controller in your application. If you do support the use of a game controller, you will need to make sure that your app has buttons contingencies for the use of the Start, Select, and Menu buttons, as not all controls include these. You will want to provide a generic gamepad controller graphic to inform your users how the controls will affect your game. You will need to ensure that your application provides controls for easily exiting your application so that the users can return to the home screen.

While networking is not a new concept for Android, the Android TV is one of the first devices that can support an Ethernet connection. As such, you will want to ensure that any networking code you have verifies that the device is connected to a network through either WiFi or an Ethernet cable.

Distributing Your Application

Once you have your app completed and you have looked over your project to make sure everything looks great, you will need to make it available for users to download. You have two major outlets here, the Google Play Store and the Amazon App Store. It is important to note that both stores have a similar approval process before your app will be accessible for users.

Google Play Store Distribution

As with most things involving the Android TV, the app publishing process with Google is fairly similar to working with a standard phone or tablet app. You will need to create an APK and sign it with a release certification, and then upload it to the Google Play Developer Console. However, when you start filling out the store listing information, you will need to go into the Android TV section and provide assets that can be used by the Play Store, as seen in Figure 6-1.

Figure 6-1. *Android TV Google Play Store listing assets*

Aside from having to provide assets, the Play Store will automatically know if you are publishing an Android TV application because of the declaration of a Leanback Launcher in your manifest file.

Amazon Fire TV Distribution

As of Fire OS 5, you are able to distribute Android apps made with the Leanback Support library and Lollipop features over the Amazon App Store for Fire TVs. While making your application compatible with the Amazon Fire OS is beyond the scope of this book, you can find detailed documentation on developer.amazon.com that goes over installing and setting up the Amazon SDK Platform tools, and how to use Amazon's specific SDK and tools in your application. This will allow you to distribute your app to an even larger group of users without much modification.

Summary

In this chapter you reviewed design and experience guidelines that have been discussed throughout this book. You have also learned about some of the ways you can distribute your application for television users. This book covered creating an application from the ground up for displaying content and helping your users enjoy media, as well as some tools that should help you with game development for Android TV. As you continue to learn about Android TV development, you should go through Google's developer documentation, watch the Google Developer videos online, and experiment with your app to find out what works best for you and your users. Good luck, and have fun!

Index

A

addAction method, 38
addVideoForDeepLink method, 80
Amazon Fire TV Distribution, 114
Android Backstage podcast, 112
AndroidManifest.xml, 23, 69, 84, 90
Android Studio module
    creation screen, 100
Android Studio project, 21–22
Android TV
  Activity option, 4
  Android devices screen, 3
  Android Studio toolbar, 6
  application, 8, 18
  game development (*see* Game
    development)
  gamepad controller, 98
  games *vs.* mobile, 89
  global search, 14
  global search
    functionality, 77, 84–85
  home screen, 10
  interactive television platform, 1
  JDK, 2
  JRE, 2
  launcher icon, 11
  layout design
    coloration, 17
    media playback app, 17
    text, 17
  live channels application, 86
  naming files, 5
  native applications, 1
  project screen, 3
  recommendations row, 12
  remote control
    application, 10–11
  systems, 23
  system images, 6
  user experience guidelines
    casual consumption, 15
    cinematic experience, 16
    simple D-pad controller, 16
  virtual device options, 6
  virtual device settings, 7
Android TV App Publishing
  Checklist, 111–112
  searching and discovery, 113
  UI design, 112
ArrayObject
    Adapter, 30, 46, 58–59, 63

B

BroadcastReceiver, 75
BrowseFragment, 24–25, 27, 65
BrowseFragment
    documentation, 29–31
buildColumnMap, 78
buildPendingIntent, 74

C

CardPresenter, 32–34
ClassPresenterSelector, 39
ConnectionRequestListener, 103
ContentProvider, 77, 82–84
ControlButtonPresenterSelector, 46

D

Data model, 25
DescriptionPresenter, 47
DetailsDescriptionPresenter, 39
DetailsFragment, 37–38
dispatchGenericMotionEvent, 96
dispatchKeyEvent, 97–98

E

entries_list_preference, 68

F

FullWidthDetailsOverview
    RowPresenter, 40

G

Game development
    achievements, 109
    controller hardware
        requirements, 98
    game controller, 113
    LAN, 99, 101–106, 108
    leaderboards, 109
    network types, 102
    quests and events, 110
Gamepad controller
    input, 90–93, 95
Generic gamepad
    controller graphics, 113
getWordMatch, 81–82
GoogleApiClient, 101, 103
Google Cast, 1
Google Play Game Services, 109
Google Play Store
    description, 98
Google Play Store
    distribution, 113–114
Gradle build system, 22
GuidedStepFragment, 86

H

HeadersFragment, 29
Hello World application, 21

I

In-App searching, 51
In-app search screen
        implementation, 60
initAction method, 38
initActions, 47
IntentService, 71

J, K

Java Development Kit (JDK), 2
Java Runtime Environment (JRE), 2

L

Layout resource file,
        activity_main, 24
Leanback feature, 23
LeanbackPreference
        Fragment, 63, 65
LeanbackPreferenceFragment
        list preference, 70
Leanback Support library, 1, 21
ListRowPresenter, 57–58
loadDatabase method, 80
loadJSONFromResource, 27–29
loadQuery method, 58
loadRelatedMedia method, 40–41
Local area network (LAN), 99
Local Search Activity
        and Fragment, 54

M

MainActivity, 23–24
MainFragment, 27
Media Player, 43–44

MediaSearchActivity.java, 54–55
MediaSearchFragment, 56–57, 61
MessageListener, 107
mRowsAdapter, 46

N

NotificationCompat.
    Builder object, 72–73
notifyArrayItemRangeChanged, 50

O

onActionClicked method, 49–50
OnActionClickedListener, 44
onActionClicked method, 42
onActivityCreated method, 27, 30
onBindDescription method, 39
onBindViewHolder, 63
onCreate method, 37, 47–48, 56, 79
onCreateViewHolder method, 64
onCreateViewHolder, 63
onEndpointFound method, 107
onHandleIntent method, 71
onItemClicked method, 60, 65
OnItemViewClicked
    Listener interface, 41
OnItemViewClickedListener, 54
Online multiplayers for real-time and
    turn-based games, 110
onMessageReceived method, 104
onSearchRequested method, 62
onSharedPreference
    Changed method, 67
OnSharedPreferenceChange
    Listener interface, 66
onUnbindViewHolder, 63

P, Q

PendingIntent, 86
Picasso library from Square, 22
Playback Control Fragment, 44
PlaybackControlsRowPresenter, 47

PlaybackOverlayFragment, 46
PlayerActivity, 42–43
PlayerControlsFragment, 43
PlayerControlsListener, 45
Playing content, 43
PreferenceCardPresenter, 64
PreferenceFragment class, 62
preferences.xml, 67

R

RecommendationService, 71–76
RECORD_AUDIO permission, 56
RecyclerView library, 22
RecyclerViews, 32

S

Saved Games API, 109
SearchOrbView, 51, 53
SearchOrbView
    onClickListener, 55–56
sendReliableMessage method, 106
Serializable, 25
setAdapter, 40
setHeadersState, 29
SettingsActivity.class, 65–66
SettingsActivity.java, 66
SettingsFragment, 66–67
setupPlaybackControlsRow, 46
SharedPreferences entry, 70
SpeechRecognition
    Callback interface, 61
SQLite database, 77–79
SQLiteOpenHelper, 78

T

TaskStackBuilder, 74
toString method, 26–27

U

Utils package, 28

V

VideoContentProvider, 83
VideoContentProvider.java, 82
VideoDatabaseHandler object, 83
VideoDatabaseHandler, 78, 81
VideoDatabaseHandler.java, 77
VideoDatabaseOpenHelper, 81

VideoDetailsActivity, 34–36, 60, 84
VideoDetailsFragment, 41–42
Video.java, 26
Video playback controls, 49

W, X, Y, Z

Wiring Up Video Details, 36

Get the eBook for only $5!

Why limit yourself?

Now you can take the weightless companion with you wherever you go and access your content on your PC, phone, tablet, or reader.

Since you've purchased this print book, we're happy to offer you the eBook in all 3 formats for just $5.

Convenient and fully searchable, the PDF version enables you to easily find and copy code—or perform examples by quickly toggling between instructions and applications. The MOBI format is ideal for your Kindle, while the ePUB can be utilized on a variety of mobile devices.

To learn more, go to www.apress.com/companion or contact support@apress.com.

Printed in the United States
By Bookmasters